David Stephen's Guide to

WATCHING
WILD LIFE

Collins · Glasgow and London

First published 1963
First published in this edition 1973
Second impression 1973

© *David Stephen 1963*
Published by William Collins Sons and Company Limited,
Glasgow and London

Printed in Great Britain
ISBN 0 00 103323 9

David Stephen's Guide to
WATCHING WILD LIFE

Michael

CONTENTS

INTRODUCTION

How OFTEN have you seen a wild fox or badger face to face? Or a stoat? Or a roe deer? And how much did you really see of any of them? Did you have a prolonged view or merely a fleeting glimpse?

Whatever your experience, you'll probably agree that mammals are far trickier to work with than birds. Birds are more easily found, easier to watch, not so difficult to outwit. Even the most elusive birds are usually less elusive than mammals.

Take a bird like the golden eagle. Almost everybody who visits the Scottish Highlands wants to see one. Many look but few ever find. Yet it is a far, far easier thing to find a golden eagle than it is to meet up with a mountain fox.

If you're told there's a certain bird in a certain place you'll find it sooner or later by the simple act of looking for it, so long as it's still there to be looked for.

This isn't so easy with a mammal. By walking through a wood you'll see this bird and that, and some of them will allow you to watch them at close range ; but you'll have to do more than just walk if you want to see something of the fox, the badger or the roe deer.

It's the same in your garden. You're more likely to find all the birds' nests before you find a single one of the field vole. And you're far more likely to see all the birds before you see the vole itself.

The mere seeing of birds can be done almost casually. Watching them for a time requires a little more care. Studying them seriously requires application and discipline, as well as some idea of what you're about.

But there's really no great difficulty in getting close to any bird subject.

Mammals aren't like that at all—as a rule. To watch them successfully you need self-discipline, a lot of patience, and some knowledge of their ways, before you'll stand much chance of seeing them for more than a few seconds at a time.

Some birds are extremely shy or cunning, or both. Many more aren't shy at all, and some will tolerate human beings at close quarters.

Birds like the raven and the hooded crow won't stand you at close range if you're in plain view. The fact that they can see you will not in itself drive them away, so long as there's a considerable distance between you and them. You won't, however, watch a mountain fox for long if you're in plain view or your scent is being carried to its nose.

Not-so-shy birds are the kind you usually find in your garden : birds like the blackbird, mavis, robins and warblers. Most of these will tolerate you at close quarters and carry on with their daily affairs. They are easily seen, easily watched and easily studied.

Then there are those birds which will literally allow you to move among them ; colonial nesters, for example.

Rooks will carry on with their affairs in the tree tops while you are sitting on the ground below. Birds like gannets and fulmars will allow you to sit and watch them from a distance of a few feet while they are on the nest.

The intimate lives of mammals aren't so easily studied. You may, and can, watch a hare or rabbits in a field while they're feeding, but it's a vastly different thing when it comes to prying into their private lives.

Some mammals are more difficult than others, just as some birds are more difficult than others. But mammals have the additional advantage of a sense of smell, so watching them is frequently a constant battle with the wind.

The things you've to contend with are : in birds, hearing and eyesight ; in mammals, hearing, sight and smell.

Though birds cannot smell, their hearing and eyesight are usually acute : in some cases exceptionally so. Mammals can see or hear well, or both ; and the one thing they can all do is smell.

My choice of mammal subjects has been based on practical considerations : those you have a chance of watching at some time. For this reason the wildcat, polecat and very small mammals have been excluded. The choice of birds had to be arbitrary : there are so many species, and only some could be included.

It's not for me, in this book, to say why you should watch the birds or mammals of the countryside, as I do. It's sufficient for my purpose that you want to do so. Whether you do it seriously, or for pleasure, is a matter for yourself. You'll certainly get a lot of enjoyment out of it.

The same thing applies to the use you may want to make of what you see. You may wish to make notes, which is a good thing to do, or you may simply wish to see. The pleasure you may derive from looking at wild creatures doesn't involve you in anything you don't want to do.

There are many books which will tell you the best ways to keep notes, the kind of notebooks to use, and so on. I don't want to use space discussing such things here. My aim is to tell in some detail how I watch wild life. A notebook of some kind is always a handy thing to have with you ; as are string, a knife, some kind of measuring tape, and a stick.

I've divided this book roughly into four sections : birds and beasts of the day, and birds and beasts of the night. But you must understand that these divisions have been made largely for convenience. Some species are active both by day and night and there is a great deal of overlapping.

MAMMALS BY DAY

ROE DEER

THE SMALL-ANTLERED roe deer is common and widespread in Scotland. In England it is scarce in some parts and common in others like Dorset, Durham, Cumberland, Lancashire and Hampshire.

The male roe deer is the buck, never a stag, and he grows antlers. The female is the doe, never a hind, and she doesn't grow antlers (except in certain rare cases which we needn't trouble about here). Young roe deer of either sex are called kids or fawns. Not calves.

An adult roebuck will stand from 2 feet 1 inch to 2 feet 5 inches at the shoulder, and weigh from 35 to 60 pounds. Bucks over 60 pounds aren't common. Does are smaller, weighing from 25 to 40 pounds when fully grown.

The summer coat of the roe deer is foxy red, short and tight. In winter, it varies through many shades of grey. Fawns, at birth, are spotted white, but the spots vanish with the change of coat in the first autumn, i.e. when the fawns are 3 months old or thereabouts. A fawn born in May should be clear of spots in late August.

In winter coat, many roe deer have a white patch on the throat and another on the gullet. These marks are very common in Scottish roe of all ages, and either sex, when they're in winter pelage.

This is something to which you might well pay attention. Information on such markings is wanted, and it would be a good thing if you made a note of all the roe deer you saw with them. At the same time, a note should be made of the time and place. It's equally important to note any deer in winter coat which don't have such markings.

The antlers of the roebuck don't often exceed 9 inches in length. They're cylindrical, and usually carry three points each. Bucks with more than three points occur from time to time and should be noted.

Antlers are made of bone and are cast and regrown each year. Adult roebucks usually cast in November.

The new antlers begin to grow almost at once, and during the growing period are covered with a furry coat called velvet. A buck at this time is said to be *in velvet*.

When the antlers are fully grown the velvet begins to strip. The buck helps the stripping by rubbing against trees and bushes. The new antlers are clear of velvet—" clean " is how we say it—from mid-March onwards. Young bucks usually cast later than old ones, and clean later. Some may be seen in velvet into May or even June.

Fawns at a year old may have no more than simple spikes, a finger or so in length. Or they may show simple forks. A few yearlings may put up a six-point head of sorts, or even a good one.

First sign of the young buck's future head-gear is the growth of the pedicles in autumn. These are rounded knobs on the skull, covered with hair, on which the antlers will grow. These knobs are often mistaken for antler buds, which they are not. The pedicles produce the antler-forming material and are never " cleaned ".

(Opposite) *Roe deer fawn about a fortnight old.*

Roebuck, showing, left to right, the pedicles, first spikes, forked head, and six-pointer head, all in velvet.

Before he grows his first real antlers, however, the young buck usually produces a hard, horny button on each pedicle. These buttons vary in size, $\frac{1}{4}$ inch to $\frac{1}{2}$ inch or so in length. Depending on a number of factors (his date of birth for one) the young buck will begin to grow his buttons as early as November or as late as the second half of December. He will rub them off at any time from mid-January until mid-February.

Now he is left with two raw sores, but these soon skin over, becoming plum-coloured. Out of the pedicles the real antlers now begin to grow and, unlike the buttons, they are covered in velvet. Growth is rapid, and the young buck will clean his first antlers in May, or thereabouts, perhaps earlier or later. It will depend on when he cast his buttons and how well he has been living.

The young buck will cast these antlers about the end of the year, and clean his second ones in spring. From then on he will follow, more or less, the usual pattern of November casting and spring cleaning.

Before you try to watch roe deer, as distinct from coming on them by chance and putting them on foot, it's as well to know something about their routine.

Buck and doe are paired in June. That is to say, the

(Opposite) *Yearling roebuck feeding on brambles in Autumn. The roe deer eats leaf, shoot and fruit of the bramble*

bucks begin to take an interest in the does on their territory.

The rut, which is the real breeding season, is in July and August.

Late in August the bucks sometimes leave the does for a time, rejoining them in October or later. From then until the spring the family group stays, more or less, together. You may even find roe in small herds of seven or eight, or more.

The break-up of the families occurs after the bucks have cleaned their new antlers (March/April) and before the fawns of the year are born (May/June). At this time young bucks may wander all over the place, while the older ones lead something of a bachelor existence until the does have new fawns at foot.

In their daily lives, roe deer are creatures of fairly regular habit. They may, indeed, spend the whole of their lives within a two-mile radius of a given place.

They feed at nightfall, during the night and early in the morning. Most of the day they spend lying up, usually in cover. Hill roe will lie in the open. But roe also feed on and off during the day, especially in quiet places, and it's a common thing to see Highland roe on the move at all hours, far from any cover.

Roe are usually referred to as woodland deer and, generally speaking, they are. But in the Scottish Highlands you'll find them regularly on the open hill, often as high as the red deer, even in winter. There they will lie out by day, and they may not seek forest cover for long periods at a time.

Where roe are present you're liable to find them in any kind of cover, but they do have their preferences.

They like young plantations, birch thickets, scrub land, or tall forest with plenty of cover. They like to be near open areas of browse or grass. They also like birch swamps and reed beds.

In winter, they like heavy cover to lie in, and in summer they will seek dense bracken or undergrowth with plenty of shade. But you'll find them on the hill in the Highlands in most months of the year.

Having placed your roe deer—that is, when you know they're present in a wood or wooded area—you have two ways of getting to know them better ; the direct and the indirect.

The first means watching deer. The second means reading their signs.

Let us consider the indirect method first.

On their home range roe deer tread out regular runways, in the open and in cover. These runs, or galleries, or racks,

Roebuck showing forked antlers in velvet.

or whatever you like to call them, become like lanes where the deer are moving in very thick cover. In winter, the animals use them when moving about in deep snow, and at such times all you may see of them are their bodies.

Roe droppings are another thing to look for. You'll find them in big lots and small lots, anywhere along the runways. Many heaps close together indicate that deer have been lying there.

Though roe droppings vary quite a lot they're not usually adherent ; that is to say each is separate. Those of a mature buck will measure about $\frac{3}{4}$ of an inch in length. But you have to be very careful identifying droppings.

You should also make a point of looking for tracks, for these can tell you a lot. To begin with, you should have the track identified for you by someone who knows roe, or examine a track after you have seen a roe pass over the ground, so that you are sure of it.

In roe deer the slot made by the feet is about $1\frac{1}{2}$ fingers wide at the heel. The fore slot and the hind one are very much alike. At walking pace, these slots will be about 15 inches apart. When roe are in flight they also print the marks of their dew claws, and these will show up on good printing surfaces like packed sand, dried silt or thin snow.

Other things to look for are :

The rings made by roe deer in certain places at mating time.

The fraying of young trees by bucks when they're cleaning their antlers in spring.

The scrapes made by bucks at the base of trees, before and during the rut.

Roe rings should be looked for in July and August. The buck does a lot of scraping at this time. Fraying of trees you would expect to find in March and April.

Generally speaking, the bigger the buck the bigger the stem he will fray on. The same is pretty well true of scrapes: the bigger the scrape the bigger the buck.

Bucks usually use young trees to fray on, the marks being up to two feet from the ground. The stems chosen will vary from thumb thickness to a bit more.

Fraying of trees also occurs during the rut. This is when the bucks will thresh tall plants (like the rosebay willow herb) and young flexible trees (usually conifers) and bushes.

This kind of behaviour you would expect in July. But before this you'll see the buck marking off his territory, drawing fence wires, branches and stems between his antlers, and leaving his scent on them.

Scraping is done with the forehooves, beside bushes, trees, or other landmarks.

During the rut roebucks sometimes fight fiercely. They approach each other with chins tucked in and antlers forward. They meet with buckled knees and lowered heads, often with great force. They will dance in circles, thrusting and pushing. And they will try to reach each other's flank.

The weaker buck usually breaks off before long. Then it is driven from the territory. Occasionally one buck wounds another. Rarely, one kills the other. Only once have I known a buck to kill his opponent.

Roe deer rings, which are used in July and August, are

usually circular in shape, though the beasts will link two together to form a figure of eight. The circle usually has some obvious object as centre : a rock, a stone, a bush, a small tree, or a clump of heather.

These rings have been much talked about in the past, and there have been many arguments about their purpose. But you can be certain of one thing about them : they're used during the rut when the buck is chasing the doe.

Roe run and mate on these rings. But they chase and mate on ground where there are no obvious rings. Ringing, in my experience, takes place both in the evening and early in the morning, around daybreak.

Roe deer are for ever chasing in circles. It's a kind of habit with them. A doe will run circles round you when you are standing beside her fawn. Fawns at play frequently do so.

On any roe ground you'll find rings of varying sizes which aren't much used, or aren't being used at all. On the other hand, you'll soon find the ones in use, the ones the deer are visiting regularly. These vary from 7 or 8 feet to 20 feet or more across. In certain cases the rings are used year after year and then inexplicably deserted.

If you want to watch roe at this time you should prepare to do so rather than leave it to chance.

I find that the best way, and the one now generally recommended by those who know roe, is to build a seat in a tree which gives a good view of the area. It's a simple matter to build such a seat, on a branch or branches about twenty feet from the ground.

Apart from the view given by a seat at such a height, there are three other advantages. You're above the deer's vision. Your scent will be out of the wind-stream reaching its nose. And any slight noise you may make at that height isn't so likely to cause alarm.

Where you're working on ground which you can reach

(Opposite) *Racing ring of roe deer, with birch tree as centre.*

easily you can prepare in advance, leaving a ladder against the tree long before the rut. You can also make your seat, or seats. Then you won't be disturbing the place at the time you should be quiet.

I don't recommend sitting on branches to watch roe deer. Unless you are a confirmed branch-sitter, such a seat quickly becomes uncomfortable, and before you know it you'll be wriggling about like an earthworm.

A small framework of 2 by 2 inch timber, with boards $\frac{5}{8}$ of an inch thick, will make a safe and comfortable seat. You can put a back on it if you like, or you can enclose it to make a hide. But, if you are prepared to go to all this trouble, you should get the work done long before the deer warm up for the rut, preferably in April or May.

You'll find it an advantage to be in position on your seat early in the morning. I like to be seated by 4 a.m. for morning watches, and two hours before sunset for evenings.

Your seat can be used at other times of the year. In the month of April I've watched deer feeding, then going to lie up for the day. I've watched them cudding. In short, your seat is a kind of watch-tower at any time.

Roe deer fawns are usually born in the second half of May and in early June, and for all practical purposes of observation you can safely take this period as normal. In my part of Scotland the last week of May is the time when most fawns are born.

There are records of fawns born in April, July and August as well, and here you can help in adding to what is known about roe deer by noting any newly born fawns you find outside the period May/June. You should make a careful note of the time and place.

(Opposite Above) *Roebuck leaping over stream. Roe are considerable long jumpers and high jumpers.*
(Opposite Below) *Roe deer doe about six years old, in winter coat.*

Twin fawns are normal in roe, but triplets also occur, so it's a good idea to note the size of any family you see.

If you see fawns still spotted with white after August you should record this fact too, because this will almost certainly mean they've been born outside the normal period.

Watching a roe doe with fawns isn't very difficult provided you take certain precautions. If you can't do it from one of your tree-top seats, you'll have to stalk into the deer.

To do this, you have to use all available cover between you and the deer, making sure that the wind doesn't carry your scent to her. Test the wind in advance of your stalk by tossing pieces of grass in the air, or by holding up a handkerchief out of sight of the deer.

No matter how much cover you have, it will be a waste of time attempting a stalk if the wind is from you to the deer.

Don't hesitate to get down on your knees, or down on your stomach. Crawl on your belly all the way if you have to. Act on the certainty that you've to approach unseen, unheard and unsmelt.

Roe deer are extremely curious and this curiosity you can sometimes turn to your advantage.

If, for example, you've reached a position which still isn't close enough to satisfy you, and you find you can't get any closer without being seen or giving the deer your wind, then you might try to bring the beast, or beasts, to you.

Keeping hidden yourself, you might try raising a white handkerchief aloft on the end of a stick, showing it momentarily, then pulling it down out of sight again.

When you're sure the deer has seen this, repeat the movement after a short interval, still keeping out of sight yourself. One or two repeats will either induce the deer to come towards you to investigate or will make her move off. If the deer comes towards you, don't try to bring her into your lap, as it were. She will not do so.

Look out for fawns from the last week of May onwards. At birth they are spotted with white, slenderly built and no bigger than hares.

Fawns may be born in woodland, in scrub, in heather, in long grass, in standing hay or corn, or on the open hill.

The behaviour of the doe will give you some guide as to the general area to be covered in your search, for she'll be near the spot at all times, and may bark at you when you're very near her young. Don't be alarmed if you meet with such a display, for this will be the full extent of her protest.

If the doe begins to run round you in circles you can be fairly sure the fawns are within a few yards of you.

Once you're sure there are fawns near you, don't go stumbling about erratically looking for them. Decide on the area you're going to search, then walk up and down in parallel lines, covering it systematically, moving slowly to give your

Roebuck showing antlers clear of velvet. This is a young animal of good body size but with a very poor head.

eyes time to scan every yard of ground ahead of you. In this way you won't miss many fawns.

While it's quite wrong to think that a doe will desert or kill a fawn which has human scent on it, you shouldn't handle fawns any more than is absolutely necessary. If you've no special need to handle the fawn it's best not to touch it at all.

Sometimes you have to touch. You may wish, for example, to weigh the fawn, or measure its height, or study it closely. But all this should be done with the minimum of handling. Do not touch if you don't have to.

If you over-handle to the point where the fawn wants to suck your thumb, you may have difficulty in persuading it to stay behind when you want to leave. And that is bad.

Where you find twins or triplets you will, as a matter of course, want to find out the sexes. Generally speaking you'll find that twins are male and female, and this is the kind of information that's useful. Note the sex ratios in all families of triplets.

Adult roe deer bark and grunt. The doe has a call to fawns like *whee-yoo*. Fawns call *Eep* or *eep-eep* or *see-ee-eep* or *peep*.

When you find a buck or doe near a fawn, you should note their behaviour. Does one of them bark at you? Or both? What do they do, if anything?

In such cases, I like to withdraw some way off, after noting where the fawns are lying, so that I can observe the family through glasses. I look for certain things. How does the doe behave now? Does she move the fawns? If so, how far does she move them? What motions does she go through, if any, to make the fawns lie down again? And, very important, what part does the buck take in all this?

The general opinion seems to be that the buck takes no obvious part in looking after his family. I have found out otherwise in two well observed cases. I have been barked

Woodland idyll : roebuck feeding at sunrise in the month of February.

at by a buck when I was looking at fawns, and observed him sniffing them afterwards. You should therefore note every possible detail of the buck's behaviour in such circumstances.

The roe fawn, in its first helpless days, is within the prey range of the fox, perhaps also of the wildcat. The golden eagle will take fawns. But the doe is a watchful mother, well able to handle any fox, and my own view is that fawns taken by foxes are more often dead than alive when found.

Outside the fawn stage the roe's only enemies are man and his dogs. But an adult buck can handle any small dog, and some bucks will face one if it is not accompanied by a man. I once found a young collie which had been stabbed to death by a roebuck during the rut.

At all times, when watching roe, you should try to find out what they're eating.

If the beasts are grazing in a field they'll be eating a lot of grass, and much the same herbage as cattle take. But, if you find them eating plants other than grass, or browsing trees and bushes, you should note as carefully as possible what is being taken. Once the animals have moved on you can check their feeding place, noting what has been eaten, and taking specimens of any plant unknown to you to have it identified.

I've found that roe can eat the foliage of the yew without apparent ill effect. I've found them eating eyebright in a field when, at first, I thought they were eating corn. They're fond of such plants as the snakeweed and the common dock. Careful notes add to our knowledge of the roe deer's food, and of any food preferences it may have.

Because roe deer are creatures of fairly regular habit, you'll eventually be able to find them on your ground almost at will. You'll expect a certain beast to be in a certain place at a certain time, unless his routine has been disturbed. And you'll soon be able to recognise individuals, and know just what ground they work over.

Marking deer is the surest way of being able to recognise individuals. The modern system is to ear-mark with coloured tabs. If you're interested in marking deer in this way you should, before doing anything on your own, discuss the matter with a professional zoologist, or make your interest known in the right place : the Nature Conservancy, for instance, the Mammal Society of The British Isles, or the British Deer Society.

RED DEER

The red deer is a much larger animal than the roe, and isn't found in so many parts of the country.

The main herds of red deer are in the Highlands and Islands of Scotland, but there are wild red deer on Exmoor, the north of England, the Southern Uplands of Scotland, and Ireland. Pockets of deer, in a few other parts, lead a precarious existence.

The red deer male is called a stag, and stands over four feet at the shoulder.

Weight varies a great deal and depends largely on feeding. A good Highland stag will weigh 18 stone clean (gutted, that is, or gralloched as they say in the Highlands); English stags will come heavier than that, and deer fed on cake and hay in winter, like park deer, will come heavier still.

The mature red deer hart has, therefore, a weight range from 12 stones to 30 stones or more.

A stag's antlers also show great variation in size, weight,

Mature red deer stag, with antlers almost full grown in the velvet, photographed on the island of Rum. Rum, which is now a Nature Reserve, is the main centre of research on the red deer, which is being carried out by the Nature Conservancy.

shape and number of points. In well-fed park specimens antlers may produce 40 points, whereas Highland stags with more than 12 points are exceptional.

Stags are usually named according to the number of tines, or points on their antlers. A stag with four on each beam will be an 8-pointer; if he has four on one and five on the other he will be a 9-pointer; if he has five on each he will be a 10-pointer. A stag with twelve points, arranged 6 on each beam to form brown, bay, tray, and 3-point top, is a Royal. Not all 12-pointer stags are Royals. A stag with 14 points is an Imperial.

Some stags never grow antlers. They are called hummels. They grow heavy and are often master stags.

The female red deer is called a hind. The young is called a calf. We speak of stag calves and hind calves.

From the calf stage to maturity the male red deer has many names, which vary according to area. For instance, a young stag with his first spikes is a knobber in the Highlands, and a pricket in England. There is no hard and fast rule.

Unlike the roe deer, the red stag casts his old antlers in the spring. He is therefore just beginning to grow his new antlers when the roebuck has his full head-gear, cleaned and hard.

The red stag cleans his new antlers in August/September.

The rut follows quickly on the cleaning of the antlers, taking place from mid-September onwards. October is usually the big month. In certain years the rut will last well into November. Frost seems to play a big part in bringing it on.

During the rut the red stag wallows in peat hags, to rise up dripping water and plastered with glaur. This the roebuck doesn't do.

The red stag grows a prominent mane which isn't found in the roebuck.

The red stag roars like a lion. The roebuck merely barks.

The red stag is a flagrant polygamist, gathering as big a harem as he can. The roebuck, if not entirely monogamous, isn't obviously polygamous.

Red deer calves are born in June. Out of season calves do occur, but late calves stand a poor chance of surviving the winter.

You will have noticed that, while the roebuck ruts in July and August, and the red stag in October, their young are born almost at the same time of year. Does the small roe deer, then, carry her young for 3 months longer than the big red deer hind?

She does and she doesn't.

In the roe deer we come up against the phenomenon known as " delayed implantation ". Growth of a young mammal doesn't begin until the fertilised egg in the mother's body becomes implanted in the wall of the uterus. In the roe deer, the eggs fertilised in July or August don't become implanted until December, when development of the young really begins. Implantation is therefore delayed for nearly five months.

Nobody knows why this should happen in the roe deer and not in the red.

If you take development from the time of implantation you get the following result :

Roe deer — mated August — delayed development until December — development begins late December — fawns end of May — development period 5 months.

Red deer—mated October—development begins at once—calves early June—development period 8 months.

Seeing red deer doesn't present the same problems as seeing roe.

If you go through a Highland glen in winter you'll almost certainly see herds feeding on the low ground, especially towards dusk. In very severe winters you'll even find them by the roadsides, often by main roads.

In summer the deer go high, so if you want to see them then you'll have to go high and, perhaps, far out, to meet up with them. But you'll still see herds and parcels of deer without much difficulty. It's getting close in to them that presents the real problem, and stalking is the way to do it.

In the Scottish Highlands, deer are stalked. Deer-stalking is a sport, with its own ethic. The rifle is the weapon used to kill deer. There is nothing in Scotland to compare with the Devon and Somerset Staghounds in England.

You may wish, when stalking red deer, to take advantage of the experience and skill of a professional stalker. The

Red deer calf, one day old, photographed in the Forest of Atholl.

best stalkers are easy men to approach and nearly always sympathetic.

On the other hand, since you're concerned with observing deer and not with killing a particular beast, you may want to do your own stalking, make your own mistakes, and learn the hard way. You can learn the hard way—make no mistake about that—but, in this instance, the hard way has no advantages over the easier way of learning from a pukka stalker.

When you come to stalking the red deer on the hill you should bear in mind the following :

Red deer have wonderful vision, and can see you a long way off. Their hearing is excellent. Their sense of smell is acute, and you can never take any liberties with a red deer's nose.

You must, therefore, plan your stalk—when you're still a long way from the deer : long before they've begun to pay attention to you, and certainly long before you've alerted them.

Let's suppose you're walking through a glen with the wind at your back and there are deer on a slope a mile and a half ahead. Obviously, you won't get near them by carrying on as you're doing, even if you get out of sight, because the wind is in the wrong direction.

You've to get down-wind from them, or at least into a position where they can't smell you.

Clearly, this means you'll have to make a detour right at the start—sometimes a very wide detour—keeping out of sight all the time until the wind is no longer from you to them. Then your stalk actually begins.

So long as you're hidden by the contours, you can walk upright, simply paying attention to the wind and keeping in mind the position of the deer.

When you've to cross open ground—a ridge-top or knowe —in view of the deer you must do it on your belly, moving

Diagram to show the importance of wind direction when stalking red deer.

forward only when all the deer have their heads down, and freezing immediately a head is raised or a beast looks in your direction.

Once you're off the exposed ground you can walk upright again. But you must be prepared to belly-crawl and freeze any time you're in view of the deer. When you run out of cover you've reached journey's end.

Why should you bother working in so close when you can watch the beasts through a telescope or binoculars? Partly, I should think, because there's more fun watching deer from a hundred yards than from half a mile, and partly because long spells of looking through a high-powered telescope don't do your eyes any good. Besides, there's the adventure of the long stalk.

Anyway, once you're close in, bear in mind that the scrape of a boot on rock may be enough to alert the deer. This doesn't mean you can't relax. You can. You're all right so long as they can't see, hear or smell you.

Stalking in this fashion is the way to get close into deer at the rut, when the stag is herding hinds and keeping them stirred up. But you must keep in mind to look out for the hinds, especially the leading hind. She's the one to watch.

This is something you'll discover very quickly for yourself. The red deer society is hind-based—a matriarchy. In any hind group, or mixed group, there's a leading female, ever on the alert, who gives the cue to every beast in the herd. So, even when you're after a master stag in charge of hinds, the hinds are the ones to be watched.

This doesn't mean to say that you can ignore the stag. You can't. Naturally, if he sees you he'll react. And his reaction won't be lost on the hinds. They'll take his word for it. But the hind is the one more likely to see you first.

In addition to the orthodox stalk, there are other ways of watching red deer.

During the rut, it's often possible to erect a watching place (like that described for roe deer) close to a wallow. You'll have to size up the possibilities for yourself, but a much-used wallow near trees has great possibilities. So has a wallow in a clearing. But get your seat up before the rut breaks. After that you can sit high and do nothing. Except wait.

A used wallow is easily recognised. It will be hoof-slotted and churned up, and there will be deer hair here and there.

Stags make a great deal of noise during the rut. They bellow, and they roar like lions. They are constantly on the move, posturing and skirmishing. They do all these things at any time of day, but they're most active at nightfall and at first light. In your high seat you'll be well placed to see much of this activity.

36

For many years I used an old ruined bothy as a hiding place during the rut. For most of the night I had beasts all round my ears. In these years I saw about everything without stirring myself beyond the doorless doorway of the bothy.

However much you see of rutting stags by day you should make a point of having a night out. You'll be amply repaid for any discomfort. You won't even know you're uncomfortable.

Always be prepared for the unexpected. Never walk right on to a knoll or ridge. Come to the crest slowly, a step at a time, so that your eyes can look before your head appears. Startled deer are lost deer as far as you're concerned. Listen, too, for the click of antlers where your eyes can't see.

Once, when I was lying in heather with a cine camera, watching hinds in charge of a 10-pointer stag, I got an unexpected shot at 6 feet when the stag almost walked on top of me. I wriggled, the stag jumped, and it was all over. But I almost had his foot in my face.

On ground now enclosed by the Forestry Commission, where the roaring of stags is now a thing of the past, I used to spend many exciting nights, over the years, during the height of the rut. I recall the night of the hummel, the 8-pointer, and the voice. . . .

It was a night of settling frost, owl-light, and the big 8-pointer stag was pacing round his harem, snorting vapour. He was thick-necked, well maned, down behind when he stopped to roar his leonine challenge to any who would listen.

The stag's stamping ground was a patch of green, former inbye, and we were watching through the glassless window of a ruined bothy.

A dark shape crossed the rough ground away below us, skirting the peat hags : an unattired stag, or hummel, far from humble. He was big, bull-headed, fat. He stopped 40 yards or so from the antlered stag and roared.

Thus began a display of threat, bluster and challenge. They paced 100 yards out, and 100 yards back, keeping their distance as though separated by an invisible barrier. Every now and again one or other would roar, and his opposite number would roar back.

Once when the 8-pointer turned his back, the hummel rushed in; but when he was still some yards away the antlered stag whipped about with head lowered to receive him. The hummel turned away and trotted to his own side of the imaginary line.

Exasperated, my companion shouted at them: " Cut out the comedy and get on with the fight! "

They listened, but didn't heed. The hinds edged away at the sound of the human voice, and the 8-pointer followed them over a knowe, leaving the hummel on his beat. The hummel then sprinted away towards another parcel of deer.

Many stag encounters are like that. Fighting is largely a formalised affair. Even a head-to-head duel is little more than a shoving match, with the victory going to the strongest shover. Occasionally stags wound each other; on rarer occasions a stag may be severely injured. Deaths are unusual. From time to time stags die when their antlers lock and they cannot separate.

A stag, rising from a wallow, dripping peat sludge and water, is an impressive sight—like a legendary monster rising from the earth. He is even more impressive when, after thrashing the heather, he runs off with a tuft snagged in his antlers. Even a hummel, despite his lack of antlers, can be an impressive beast during the rut. Hummels, in fact, are often master stags.

A master stag looks what Landseer called him: the monarch of the glen. But his reign is brief. He can't last out the rut. Other stags take over in succession as the earlier ones are run out. After the rut the heyday of the stags is over, and they retire to live quietly while they recuperate from the drain on their strength.

Hinds can be watched without much difficulty when they have young calves, because they won't go very far from the places where the calves are lying.

Once you've discovered a few calves you can withdraw some distance, hide yourself, and study the hinds through a telescope.

Calves aren't so difficult to find, despite the vastness of the ground. Hinds, on good hind ground, have their favoured calving places, so that you can find the young ones in much the same neighbourhood year after year. This is especially so on heavily stocked deer forests. By studying the ground at calving time you can pick your watching place early.

You can watch the hinds nursing their calves, putting them down, striking them up and generally mothering them. You will also observe, sooner or later, that one hind may stay behind to keep an eye on all the calves of her group while the other mothers are away grazing.

A hind will move a calf to a new lying-up place after she discovers that it has been touched by human hands. She won't desert or kill it, as so many people seem to think.

When you come on a calf for the first time, you should stop short of it, and stand still, just watching it. The calf, completely aware of your presence, will behave in a typical way.

It will lie perfectly still.

It will breathe slowly, its flank heaving only slightly.

It will blink its eyes as little as possible, so that you may begin to wonder if it is stuffed or real.

This kind of behaviour is instinctive in a deer calf. The habit of lying still means that the calf is overlooked by animal

Red deer stags, in velvet, photographed by flashlight.

enemies like the fox, the wildcat and the eagle, who recognise form only in movement.

If the calf is very young it won't even respond to your touch, at least at first. If you persist in your attentions it will eventually become friendly, suck your thumb, and even follow you. This is bad. You shouldn't do this to a calf.

The calf does all these things because it hasn't yet learned that Man is an enemy.

You might well try an experiment concerning this handling. Stroke the calf several times with your hand, so that you leave plenty of your scent on it, then go away and watch until the hind has moved it. You will often find that its behaviour is quite different the next time you visit it. It will show fear ; it may scream ; it may run off. This doesn't always happen, but there's no doubt that the calf is a different animal once the hind has visited it and found man-smell on it.

Red deer, when shifting ground, have their favourite routes. In difficult country the contours may compel them to take particular routes, through gorges or over ridges. In such cases, when you've observed their habits and marked out the ground, you can sometimes lie up and wait for them to come to you.

There is, of course, another way to bring deer to a chosen spot, and that is to bait them. This works well in a hard winter. It used to be the custom to feed deer in many forests. The beasts would gather in winter to feed on hay and other foods. Baiting is simply a variant of this.

Deer, left to their own devices, quite often find their own way to winter food supplies—turnips and so on—and in such cases they are a nuisance to the farmer. But such behaviour presents you with a ready-made way of observing deer. All you've to do is to hide nearby before the deer come.

In Highland deer forests the red deer move quickly and readily up and down through the contours, their movements being largely dictated by weather and food supply.

They also have their summering ground and their wintering ground and the two may be many miles apart.

It is essential, therefore, on any forest, to get to know these movements, which you can learn by experience if you have the time, or very quickly from the stalker if you ask him. A deer forest in the Highland sense, is the ground occupied by deer, even when it is bare of trees.

In very hot weather the deer go high for coolness, and to escape the flies.

Storms will bring them down in summer almost as readily as snow will in winter.

Generally speaking, however, the beasts live high, and far out, in summer, and low, and close in, in winter.

During prolonged snow you can expect to find the red deer down in the glens in the evenings, scraping through for a bite. In the forenoon and afternoon they'll lie on the ridges, catching whatever sun there is; or in sheltered places if a storm is blowing.

In summer it's a good plan, and a fine experience, to spend at least one night on the high ground among the deer.

If you choose your spot well—that is, if you're concealed and down-wind of the place where you know the deer to be—you'll see something of the idyllic side of the red deer's spartan life.

The eagles are at rest. The ravens are silent. On the hill an owl may hoot, or skirl its hunting cry. But the night will really be to the deer, and the sounds you're most likely to hear are the bark of a hind or the couthie baa-ing of a calf.

It's a relaxing thing, a kind of meditation, to lie out on a fine night while the hinds graze the rain-washed alpine grass, and the calves skip and bleat.

Placed thus, you'll realise what a watchful beast the red deer hind really is: how every sound, movement, or drifting shadow attracts her attention; how she throws up her head, swivels her ears and flares her nostrils, so that all her senses seem to be working co-operatively. She misses nothing. Except you.

Just always bear in mind that hind groups are, if anything, more difficult to outwit than stag groups.

In calf-hood, the red deer's enemies are foxes, wildcats

42

and eagles. But it's doubtful if any of them really kills many calves.

This is something you can check for yourself by watching calves which are on the hunting range of a pair of golden eagles. You can then cross-check your observations by looking at the eagles' eyrie to see if any calves have been brought in.

On eagle ground you should make a particular point of watching over any still-born deer calf you may come across. Experience has taught me that this is the likeliest calf to find its way into an eyrie. If you're lucky, you may be present when an eagle flies down to such a calf, and then you'll see how she deals with it.

It's worth noting that hinds frequently drop their calves near an eyrie, right under the eagle's flight line. I've seen calves dropped at distances of 40, 100 and 400 yards from an occupied eyrie, right on the eagle's fly-in route.

Where deer are not being constantly disturbed, or where, as in the Scottish Highlands, they're disturbed only at certain times, they're not notably nocturnal in habits, and will feed and move about by day.

In the Highlands, the stalking season is now from 1st July to 20th October (stags) and from 21st October to 15th February (hinds) This is in keeping with long tradition. Night poachers take deer at any time.

I mentioned red deer stags wallowing during the rut. In fact wallowing takes place at other times, and both sexes wallow.

Master stag wallowing in peat hag during the rut.

When deer are changing their winter coats in the period April/May you'll find old hair in and around wallows, indicating that the habit is an aid to getting rid of the old coat.

Young beasts wallow, too, and it isn't an uncommon thing, at the period of the rut, to find a knobber rolling after a master stag has emerged plastered with wet peat.

It's a good plan to examine all the cast antlers you find on the hill. Measure them, weigh them, and check the number of points on each. Antlers vary a great deal in weight, texture, number of points and spread, so if you make some

*Red deer heads showing, left to right, first spikes, six-pointer,
royal stag.*

notes, instead of trusting to memory, you'll be able to check
the differences in different places.

Hinds eat cast antlers. So do stags. This isn't so
surprising as it may seem. Antlers are made of bone.
Growing them is a big drain on the stag's calcium resources.
So he will eat them after he has cast them. Hinds are
especially fond of chewing old, weathered antlers.

A word about what you should wear when after deer.

Clothing which blends with the background is best. You
should avoid bright colours, or plain white. Soft tweed is
best. Waterproofed materials scrape and rustle, and shouldn't
be worn in dense cover or when you're close in to your deer.

Any stout boot will do for the hill, so long as you're able
to walk reasonably quietly. People who don't have this
knack should wear a rubber sole of the Commando type,
which won't scrape against rocks. I wear light-weight boots
of the Veldtschoen type, with tacketed soles.

Binoculars are excellent for close and medium distances,
and are all you're likely to need. But for long range spying
a good telescope is advisable. Remember that long viewing
through a high-powered glass isn't easy on the eyes.

The use of hides for watching red deer on the hill is something
you'll have to decide and work out for yourself. There's no
rule, except the following :

Deer will shy away from a strange object. Moving upwind as they do when feeding they'll move on to your hide in this way if they're suspicious. A hide should therefore be part of the landscape with which the deer are already familiar.

Fixtures are best: old bothies, ruins, rocks, cairns. If you're close to forest, get up a tree.

Always bear in mind that, once you put your deer on the move, they may go right out of sight before stopping. If not unduly alarmed, they may not go far, but they'll be alert and suspicious for some time afterwards.

Deer crossing your front can sometimes be halted, for a short spell, by giving them a calf call.

If you're approaching deer by car, as is often possible in the Highlands, you'll find they won't run off so long as the car keeps moving. They may stay for a bit even if the car

Red deer moving up from the low ground in mid-winter.

Part of the experimental herd of reindeer at Rothiemurchus, Inverness-shire. This herd is now thriving and most of the animals in it are now Scottish-born.

comes to a stop, so long as the slow-down is gradual. They'll almost certainly run if the car stops abruptly, and certainly when a door is opened. All this is with regard to deer which have the car in view.

Deer will pass quite close to a car which has been parked for some time, and which they've been seeing for some time —providing doors haven't been opening and closing, and people haven't been popping in and out.

In other words, a car is an excellent observation post if you're prepared to sit in it, perhaps for some hours, and do nothing except wait.

Here now is a rough guide to the red deer's yearly cycle.

During the winter, the sexes live mostly in separate herds : stag groups and hind groups.

During March and April, sometimes later, the stags cast their old antlers.

The growing of the new antlers goes on through April, May, June and July, into August. The most forward stags then clean their antlers, but cleaning goes on well into September.

Hinds give birth to calves mostly in the first half of June.

In September the rut begins, and as it reaches its height you'll find groups of hinds in charge of a single master stag.

In November (usually) the groups break up, the masters retiring to recuperate, and the stags and hinds forming separate herds again.

When in search of deer you should always bear in mind that other types are liable to appear in certain places : the Japanese Sika, the Fallow, the Muntjac, and, of course, the Siberian Roe.

The Siberian Roe may be seen in such places as Bedfordshire and Buckinghamshire, in which areas the Muntjac is also well established.

The Japanese sika may be found in Inverness and Argyll.

The fallow deer is present in many parts of the country, in a more or less wild state. Perthshire is one such place.

In addition to these, there are other species which have escaped and gone wild. It's advisable therefore to look twice at any beast which isn't obviously a native. The sika can be easily confused with the red deer, so you should look at as many photographs of both as you can.

HARES AND RABBITS

There are three species of hare in the British Isles : the brown hare, the mountain hare, and the Irish hare.

Outside Ireland, the species familiar to most people is probably the brown hare of the low country. The mountain hare isn't so widely distributed ; it's a beast of the higher ground and the mountains. But it would be a great mistake to think there's a hard line of demarcation between the two.

In many places their ranges overlap.

Since myxomatosis cleared the rabbits from hill areas the brown hare has been moving into the glens, and on to higher ground. It has been seen on Ben-y Gloe, in Perthshire, where no one can remember ever seeing it before.

By and large, however, the brown hare is an inhabitant of low, rolling country and grassland.

The mountain hare is a native of the Scottish mountains. It has been introduced into Ireland, Wales and England. It differs from the brown hare in having shorter ears, and a shorter tail, with no black on its upper surface. It changes to white in winter.

The Irish hare is a native of Ireland, but has been introduced at different times into Wales and Mull. Bigger than the mountain hare, it's smaller than the brown. It doesn't change to white in winter, but its winter coat is greyer than the summer.

Let us look at the brown hare.

It's a creature of habit. It has its favourite exits from fields—by a gateway, a hole in a wall, or a gap in a hedge— and for that reason is fairly easy to poach.

You'll learn
a lot about the habits of
brown hares by watching a good
poacher at work. Or by talking to him.

For the brown hare, the main period of activity
(the mating period) is in spring—in March. That's when
the hare, traditionally, goes mad. Or seems to.

But it would be a mistake to think this behaviour is confined
to March. It isn't. March is the month when it's most
obvious. Depending on the kind of spring it is, the madness
may begin earlier or later.

That the brown hare mates at other times is obvious from
the fact that leverets can be found from March to September.

Spring hares box, and jump, and caper all over a field. The
males box each other, and females will box males to
discourage their attentions. With field glasses, you can
watch all this from the roadside, or from behind a hedge.
You may even see the facial expressions. But you won't hear
the grunts and hisses. You'll want to be closer for that.

If the beasts are posturing in a field which has scattered
trees—parkland for example—the best thing to do is to get
into a tree. Trees are the greatest watching places of all.
So few four-footed creatures look up.

Jack hares take no part in family affairs. The doe rears
the young on her own.

52

Leverets are born furred, and with their eyes open, above ground. After birth, each moves a little way off to a form, or lying-up place, of its own. This spreading of the family reduces the risk of total loss by predators. A fox, for instance, has to seek for them all individually.

The doe hare visits her young periodically, calling them to her to nurse. Evening, during the night, and early morning, are the usual times. But a hare will visit her young during the day if she isn't being disturbed.

Though it's difficult to get near a hare with leverets in an open field, it isn't if she has them near a wall or a hedge or a tree. You can either climb into the tree, or lie behind the wall or hedge.

You can even build, nearby, a hide of straw, or branches, on a

framework of netting, but there's no guarantee you'll get away with it. On the other hand you will, sometimes.

If you find very young leverets in the evening, it can be worth while to stay up and wait for daylight, if you can get up a tree nearby. During darkness, you can use a red torch. The hare will pay no attention to it.

You should try hard to get close to a hare with young. This is much more satisfactory than watching through glasses, though it won't teach you much more about hares. Except the intimate sounds made by doe and young.

The hare is most attentive to her young. But she soon leaves them. She teaches them nothing. A hare will carry a leveret as a cat carries a kitten.

While they are dependent on her the hare will defend her leverets boldly, sometimes with unexpected savagery. I've watched one drive off sheep who came too close. I've seen another chase a curlew. And I've seen one face a stoat in defence of her young, kicking out at the small marauder with her big, hairy hindfeet.

A hare returning to her young will break her line, so that she cannot easily be followed by a predatory nose. Once, when I was tracking a hare in snow, I found three big breaks in the trail, which then ran along the top of a dry-stone wall. From this, after fifty yards, the hare made a great leap towards a tree in the field. Below the tree I found her small leverets, all dead.

Snow, of course, betrays the movements of the hare, and you should make full use of it.

If a hare has leverets near an outhouse, or building, you have as good a watching place as that provided by a tree.

After a fall of snow, look for the tracks of a hare. New tracks. Follow them until you grow tired, or until you catch up with the hare.

How far has it travelled? Did any tracks join it? Or did

(Opposite) *Leveret of the brown hare, about one week old.*

you find blood in the snow? Tracking for its own sake is a pastime to be recommended. By their tracks you will find out what they do.

Make an opportunity of seeing a greyhound coursing a hare. You may not like it, but you'll learn something about hares.

Go out with a good poacher. See him use net and snare. You may not like either, but you'll learn something.

Go beagling as an observer. If you're a beagler you'll go anyway. In either case you'll learn about hares.

Go to a mountain hare drive in Scotland if you can. When these hares become too numerous, they're driven down, and shot. It's part of the mountain hare's life, so you should see it. Even if you don't like it.

In short, when you're after hares, explore every avenue that may lead to hares. You don't have to go the same way again if you don't want to.

The mountain hare is blue in summer, white in winter. The white coat makes it difficult to see when there's snow on the ground, but as often as not you'll find it on ground clear of snow (where it feeds) and then it's as obvious as it could possibly be.

This species also has its gatherings, as you can tell from the fur you find lying about where the beasts have met.

Unlike the brown hare this species often seeks cover, so it can be looked for hiding in peat hags or cuttings, under banks, and in holes. It will readily seek such cover when pressed. During snow storms mountain hares will shift ground in a body.

This hare is a common prey of the golden eagle and the mountain fox.

Before myxomatosis, the rabbit was found almost everywhere in Britain except on the tops of mountains—sometimes in small groups, often in large colonies. It was looked upon as one of the commonest animals in the country.

The European rabbit was brought to England by the Normans. Probably it came originally from Spain. It was the 19th century before it began to colonise, with the help of man, the mainland of Scotland. It became a major pest of agriculture and forestry, and may become so again. It became a common prey item for many predators—eagle, buzzard, fox, wildcat, marten, stoat, badger and others—which they are now having to learn to do without.

Nowadays, rabbits are only a remnant of their former numbers, although in some areas they're staging what appears to be a successful comeback. This may be due in part to the immunity of individuals, or a reduction in the killing power of the myxoma virus which causes the disease.

Although the rabbit is a burrowing animal it will also be

found lying out. Indeed, many present-day rabbits appear to be confirmed outliers, especially where numbers are low. Where they're coming back, most of them are in burrows. Outlying rabbits are difficult, if not impossible, to study at close quarters. Rabbits in burrows present no problem at all.

The obvious way to watch rabbits at a warren is to build a hide right in the middle of them. It should be built on strong uprights, and raised from 6 to 9 feet above the ground. The rabbits will accept it quickly and forget about it in a couple of days.

Make the actual hide of wire netting and hessian, and cover it over with bundles of grass or other vegetation. I've watched a doe with young from a platform hide draped with long stalks of rank rhubarb.

On this platform you'll be above the rabbits' heads which means you'll be out of their noses. This is essential, because their sense of smell is good. But their hearing is also good, so you'll have to sit still.

If there's a good tree handy to the warren you could get into it and save yourself the trouble of building a platform.

Or, if you prefer it, you can sit well back and watch through glasses, but this isn't nearly so good. At night it's useless.

Where rabbits are in warrens you'll find individuals sitting about at all times of the day. You'll find rabbits feeding by day where they're not being unduly disturbed. But dusk and dawn are the really active periods.

So you can use your hide during the day, early in the morning, or in the evening. I've found the best times to be in a hide are an hour before dawn and an hour before sunset. A lot happens in the two hours following.

Rabbits spread out quickly once they've emerged to feed, but you can hold them in for a time by baiting with a proprietary brand of rabbit pellets. You can put these down in small heaps here and there, in the afternoon for the evening watch and before dawn for the morning watch.

Wild rabbits are very fond of these pellets, so you can have the whole warren round your ears if you bait carefully.

Young rabbits, almost one month old, at the mouth of their nursery burrow, or " stop ".

From your hide, which the rabbits are now ignoring, you can observe their behaviour—feeding, posturing, chasing, fighting. Pay attention to the order of emergence after you've chased all the rabbits underground. Is there any order? Does a buck appear first? Or a doe? Or young animals?

Evening after evening I've watched the same burrow, and seen the young animals come out first, then a doe, and then a buck. I've seen the doe out first at times, but never the buck. Yet it has been said a buck always leads. The only time I've seen a buck leading was in a race for safety when danger threatened. Obviously, much depends on circumstances. This is an aspect you can keep in mind when you're watching a colony.

The breeding season in rabbits is the first half of the year.

Rabbits which litter after the end of June are usually young females born at the beginning of the same year.

In the wild rabbit we meet the phenomenon of resorption. A percentage of litters conceived—sometimes a high percentage—is not born. Instead, after a period of development, the young die in the uterus and are resorbed through the mother's tissues. This is a brake on the potential output of young rabbits.

Rabbits, like hares, practise what is known as refection. That is to say they re-swallow the first pellets passed through the bowel. These are subsequently voided as the hard droppings we know so well. It isn't too great a stretching of the facts to say that the rabbit, in effect, chews the cud. But not in the same way as deer or cattle.

Rabbits make no nests except for young, and only does make nests. The nest is usually placed at the end of a short burrow away from the warren, but may be in a side pocket of a burrow in the warren. It is made of dried grass, mixed with wool which the doe plucks from her body.

Once in a while you'll find a nest above ground, woven into a rush clump or grass tussock.

You can watch a nesting burrow—" stop " it is called—from a nearby tree or a raised platform, and you should make a point of doing so at the first opportunity.

The doe spends a lot of time with her young when they're small and naked. Later she visits them from dusk till daylight. Before their eyes are open she may lie up with them well on towards noon. Much depends on the amount of disturbance. But, in any case, a stop is easy to watch.

You'll see the doe unseal the entrance to the stop when she arrives, and pat the earth back to reseal it when she leaves. Almost invariably she'll leave a tell-tale wisp of wool.

When the young are near weaning you'll see them playing outside the stop with the doe. Or on their own. I've

Wild rabbit adults and young animals photographed at their burrow which has been baited as described in the text.

watched, and photographed, young ones at a stop from a distance of 8 feet.

When you're watching a stop, you may just be lucky enough to see it raided by some predator—like a fox. Foxes dig out a lot of young rabbits. Before daylight you may see a badger. The digger may be a hedgehog. There's always the possibility of the unexpected.

Take an opportunity to go out with someone using ferret and purse nets. You'll learn about rabbits. Or go out with a long-netter. There aren't so many of them now, rabbits being too thin on the ground to make this method worthwhile. Watch a good snarer setting snares. You don't know the rabbit until you've seen all these things.

SQUIRRELS

There are two squirrels in Britain to-day —the native red and the alien grey. Usually, where the grey moves in the red moves out. It isn't that the grey squirrel actually kills the red ; it simply takes over the ground and holds it. Once the grey is established the red seems to be unable to get a foothold again, and it is to-day a scarce animal in much of England.

The grey squirrel is a pest, ruthlessly hunted by foresters, market gardeners and others, and for a while the Forestry Commission paid a bounty for every grey tail. The bounty has stopped but the war still goes on. A further reason for the grey squirrel's unpopularity is that it displaces the native red species.

In some areas you'll find only grey squirrels ; in others only red. In a very few others you'll find both species on the same ground.

Both species tame quickly, and in public parks, Zoological Gardens, and such places, soon learn to come to visitors for food. The truly wild squirrel is a shy, elusive beast, who prefers to view people from behind the trunk of a tree, where he can't be seen. But the wild beasts can be taught to appear where you want them.

(Opposite, above) *Grey squirrel feeding.*

(Opposite, below) *Pine cones which have been eaten down by grey squirrel. Uneaten cone is also illustrated for comparison.*

This is done by baiting. Most animals can be attracted to some kind of food which they like. At a selected spot in a wood or forest, where you know there are squirrels, you lay out food on tree stumps and on the ground. Nuts, pieces of chocolate, raisins and such food make good bait. Nearby you have a hiding place, where you can sit still, unseen, and watch. All you have to do is slip into this hiding place at a moment when no squirrels are about, and wait.

I've filmed the red squirrel in this way, and there's no doubt at all that you'll see more squirrels by sitting down than by walking around. Wild squirrels, that is.

Squirrels breed in the spring. Their nest, called a drey, is built in a tree, and you might well mistake it for a bird's nest. You can, of course, climb up and make sure ; or you can watch to see if a squirrel is visiting it.

A good time to watch squirrels is when the young are making their first outings in the branches. All you've to do is sit still and look up. Binoculars will be a help.

Both squirrels will come to a bird table, and take almost any food available. Both will raid the garden, and may become a nuisance. Either will take eggs or nestlings of small birds, and you may find yourself wishing you'd never encouraged such attractive rascals as squirrels.

The grey squirrel is American, and provides a good

example of the dangers of introducing exotic species. From being a mere escapee it has become the dominant squirrel, in some places reaching plague numbers. It learns quickly to tolerate people who tolerate it, and if encouraged in the garden will soon be in the house.

Main predators on squirrels in this country are martens, foxes and cats, wild or tame. The pine marten, which can kill them in the trees or on the ground, is confined to a few of the wilder parts of the north-west and central Highlands. The wildcat, too, is confined to Scotland. So neither makes much impact on the squirrels of Britain as a whole.

Squirrels don't hibernate, although they'll lie up for days at a time during wild weather. But you'll see the red squirrel out on freezing days, when there's deep snow lying, so long as the weather is sunny.

The red squirrel makes an interesting pet ; but bear in mind that it can be very destructive in the house, and that it won't hesitate to bite people it doesn't like, or any time it takes the notion.

The squirrel leaves the remains of his meals lying about to betray his presence. Thus you will learn about the presence of squirrels from the presence of nut shells, or cores of pine cones, scattered about under the trees. You may find the remains of several hundred cones on a few square yards.

MOLES

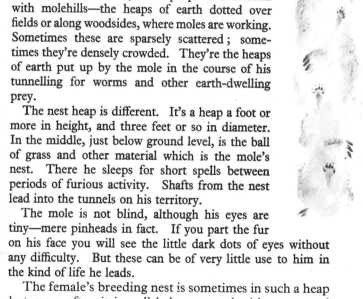

The common mole, moudie, or moudiewart, is an animal which nearly everybody knows but which nearly everybody hasn't seen alive and free. This is because it lives almost entirely underground, and isn't often seen above ground by day.

On the other hand, most people are familiar with molehills—the heaps of earth dotted over fields or along woodsides, where moles are working. Sometimes these are sparsely scattered ; sometimes they're densely crowded. They're the heaps of earth put up by the mole in the course of his tunnelling for worms and other earth-dwelling prey.

The nest heap is different. It's a heap a foot or more in height, and three feet or so in diameter. In the middle, just below ground level, is the ball of grass and other material which is the mole's nest. There he sleeps for short spells between periods of furious activity. Shafts from the nest lead into the tunnels on his territory.

The mole is not blind, although his eyes are tiny—mere pinheads in fact. If you part the fur on his face you will see the little dark dots of eyes without any difficulty. But these can be of very little use to him in the kind of life he leads.

The female's breeding nest is sometimes in such a heap but more often it is well below ground with no mound directly overhead. The nest is made mainly of grass packed into a tight ball. Young are born in early summer. At first

Opposite) *Mole feeding on earthworm.*

Working heaps of the mole on pasture-land.

they are blind and naked, but their fur soon grows.

The mole, besides being, for his size, one of the most powerful animals on earth, is one of the world's great gluttons. He rests between bouts of eating and drinking. His main food is earthworms, which he eats round the clock. An eight-hour fast would be the death of him.

When eating a worm the mole passes it into his jaws with

his feet, the strong claws of his forepaws scraping it partly clear of earth and slime as they pass it along. This you can study by keeping a mole for a day or two. If you do keep a mole remember to leave him enough food to keep him going through the night when you're in bed. Luckily, the mole does well on some of the modern cat foods, at least for a few days, so you can supplement the worm supply with this.

What weight of food will your mole eat in a day? How long does it take a mole to dig himself out of sight? Will he eat a dead mouse? Or vole? Or another mole?

Good times to catch moles are at spring ploughing, and when potatoes are being dug. Then they are often turned out of the ground and can be caught. Taking moles in mid-summer is not to be recommended as you may be taking a female who is nursing young. A mole will bite, so be careful how you handle it.

One thing you can find out with your captive mole is how quickly these animals can move on the surface of the ground. Put one down on tarmac or concrete (so that it can't dive into the ground) and you'll discover you've to move faster than a walk to keep up with it.

You can observe how the mole moves through the earth by packing soil between two upright sheets of glass, about four inches apart, and putting the mole between them. He'll usually travel along against one sheet or the other, so you really see him in a sectioned tunnel. When you're finished with him, release your mole where you found him.

Moles are most often seen above ground (and that isn't very often) in spring when males are chasing each other, after a shower of rain which brings up the worms, and in ditches when they're up for a drink of water. Moles drink a great deal of water, and always have a tunnel leading to a supply, or near a supply.

But the mole, like other small mammals—shrews, voles and mice—isn't an easy subject to watch in the field : not because he's difficult in himself but because of where he lives. It's sometimes possible to keep, say, a woodmouse or a dormouse under observation for brief spells when you know her nest. But the small mammals are most easily watched in captivity.

If you want to learn something about the study of these small mammals in the field you should make the acquaintance of a zoologist who is live-trapping and marking them for population studies. The body to get in touch with is the Mammal Society of the British Isles.

GREY SEALS

Grey seals are marine mammals who have to come ashore to breed. In Britain they've a number of breeding stations, notable ones being North Rona, the Orkneys and the Farnes. Their breeding season is September and October, into November. They'll haul out on skerries and such places at other times—when moulting for example—but the main landing season is the breeding season.

Male seals are bulls; females are cows. But the young aren't calves : they're pups. And the breeding station is a rookery, not a sealery.

Seal pups are white at birth. The cows suckle them for two

or three weeks, then desert them to join the bulls. The young seal puts on weight at an incredible rate and is soon rolling in fat. A pup weighing 30 pounds at birth may scale 90 pounds at the age of three weeks. Pups begin to moult, and assume their first adult pelage at about the age of three weeks.

The only problem about seeing seals is the physical one of getting to the rookery You may have to go up and down cliffs, or sail many miles to island rookeries. In the latter case tides and heavy seas have to be taken into account. The seals themselves aren't difficult to get to grips with.

But bear in mind, when you're walking among seal pups lying on a beach, that these same pups can bite savagely and severely. So you shouldn't handle a pup unless you're very fully aware of what you're doing, and the risks involved. Like everything else the risks become slight as know-how increases.

Where the seals are lying well inland, as they are at some breeding stations, notably North Rona, they can be watched from a reasonable distance without disturbing them or causing any reaction.

Where the pups are on the beaches, as they most frequently are, the cows will be swimming about offshore, and will come ashore only to suckle their pups. In this case the best plan is to get down among the rocks and stay there. Before long you'll see seals coming ashore to their pups, seals bobbing about in the water close at hand, perhaps seals hauling out at your elbow. But a sudden move will send them all back into the water.

Obviously the breeding season is the best time to watch seals ; then you know where to find them and you know that they'll stay close at hand. But seals come ashore to rest after spells of fishing, and they come ashore to breed. Many of these hauling out places are traditional, and seals can be watched there. Part of the Farne Island group, for instance, is used by seals outside the breeding season.

During the past few years the grey seal has been the centre of great controversy. Young animals from the Farnes and Orkneys have been causing damage to salmon nets. Many complaints have come from the Tweed area. It isn't so much the actual damage to the nets that matters; the important thing is the number of salmon which escape through the holes made by the seals. The whole problem is being investigated, and a trial culling programme has begun in Orkney.

Before a solution is found the methods of taking salmon may have changed so much that culling will become unnecessary. Nobody knows. The one certainty is that seals make no significant impact on the sum total of British salmon stocks. This ties up with what is known about most predator-prey relationships.

Close-up of grey seal pup aged about 3 weeks.

BIRDS BY DAY

THE RAREST breeding bird in Great Britain (if you forget the goshawk) is almost certainly the osprey. For many years there was only one known pair—at Boat of Garten in Inverness-shire. Now there are several, including a pair at Loch of Lowes. These two pairs, both closely guarded, are visited by thousands of people each year.

Despite its rarity, the osprey has probably been looked at by more people, at one time and in one season, than any other bird of prey—which is why it is included here. The Royal Society for the Protection of Birds has brought the public to the ospreys, by providing a hide for them about

200 yards from the nest. This is mass viewing, and there's been a lot of criticism of the idea. But the birds do not suffer. The public has been made osprey conscious. And it's better, I believe, to see ospreys in this way than not to see them at all.

Ospreys were once common enough in Scotland, but in the 19th century they were shot and harried out of existence, a leading part being taken in the extermination of breeding stock by men like the notorious Charles St. John.

For fifty years no osprey was known to have bred successfully in Britain. Now there's a single pair in Scotland. It remains to be seen if there will be others.

The osprey is a fishing hawk, and in North America is known as the fish-hawk. It's a bird you won't be in doubt about for long, because it plunges into water to catch its fish as a kestrel dives to earth to catch mouse or vole.

If there are ospreys in a neighbourhood the place to look out for them is at a likely fishing loch, where all you need to do is sit still in some kind of cover, with binoculars handy.

The nest of the osprey is built right on top of a tree, usually a conifer, and very often a dead or dying one. The chosen tree may be in forest, but it's much more likely to be an isolated one, or one of an isolated group. This means that nest-building isn't difficult to confirm, and observe. It also means that the nesting birds can be easily watched. As a result the Royal Society for the Protection of Birds has been able to introduce the public to the osprey, in a way that would have been impossible with birds in a forest. The Society's main problem was keeping egg collectors away from the nest at night, and this was accomplished by having microphones at the nesting tree, a listening post close at hand, and round-the-clock guards.

The biggest bird of prey in the British Isles is the golden eagle. Scotland has practically all the British eagles, and

(Opposite) *Fully-fledged golden eaglet displaying at the author.*
Although eaglets can look fierce, they can, with a little care, be handled
easily at this stage.

almost all of them are in the Highlands and Islands. In recent years the birds have nested in Ireland and southern Scotland; but so far Wales and England haven't been colonised.

You're not likely to confuse the eagle with any other bird, except, perhaps, the buzzard. Of course, the eagle is bigger, but this isn't much of a help with a single bird, flying high, when you've nothing to compare it with.

Experience will eventually enable you to tell which bird you're looking at, but there are certain rule of thumb methods of identification you can use right away.

Birds feeding on the highway, perched on roadside fence posts or telephone poles, circling around you at low altitudes, or flying in circuses, will almost always turn out to be buzzards. The buzzard is the noisy one, often calling for long periods; the eagle is rather a silent bird. In silhouette, the buzzard appears to have no neck; the eagle has an obvious neck. In addition the eagle is a very dark bird compared with the average buzzard.

Although golden eagles are mountain birds, they don't nest on the tops of mountains.

Most eyries in the Scottish Highlands are between 1,000 and 2,000 feet above sea level. You'll find some over 2,000, and in certain western isles you'll find them under 500 feet. An eyrie may be inaccessible, or it may be one into which you can walk.

There are tree eyries on the mainland of Scotland, but most are on ledges of cliffs or crags, usually with a rock overhang giving some kind of shelter from above. Most eyries are known to somebody, and in any area there will always be someone who can tell you all the likely nesting places. You can chart them yourself from an Ordnance Survey Map.

Eagles usually have two or three eyries which they use in

Cock golden eagle arrives at eyrie carrying a rowan branch.

turn ; but you can't be sure of an orderly sequence, or a flitting every year. A great deal depends on the weather at nesting time. For example, an eyrie filled with snow when the hen is ready to nest will be by-passed.

Eagles nest early in the year—after the middle of March ; and it's in March that you can watch an eyrie being made up. But you can't sit on a golden eagle's doorstep and expect the birds to carry on with their work. Unless you're well hidden they certainly won't. The safest way is to find a vantage point, some distance away, where you can sit quietly and watch the birds through binoculars or telescope.

The more open the approach to an eyrie the further you'll have to stay back. With eagles, you've to think of distances, not in terms of yards, but in terms of hundreds of yards. Depending on conditions you may have to get a mile away.

The golden eagle needs a lot of territory, but size varies. On Lewis, in the Outer Hebrides, nine pairs have been recorded on 100,000 acres.

A scouting eagle isn't an easy bird to catch up with. There's the problem of discovering his timetable, his routes and his favourite resting places.

Regular walking round, or through, an eagle's territory will certainly bring you to grips with the bird from time to time ; but if you choose a vantage point which gives you a wide view of the ground you'll often do better simply by sitting still in one place. Meeting an eagle is easier still if the birds are feeding on carrion. On Lewis, for example, many eagles feed on mutton carrion, and the easiest way to see one there (at close quarters) is to keep watch near a dead sheep on which it has been seen feeding.

If you visit an eyrie while the hen is still on eggs, you should make a quick turnabout, and clear right out of sight immediately afterwards—choosing an open exit so that the birds can see that you've left. During such a visit you can identify quickly any prey you see lying about, and recover any pellets lying readily to hand. These you can examine later, when you're off the ground.

Once the young have hatched you'll have a little more time to look about for pellets and prey remains.

You can also take a look at what's lying in the nest, and make a note of it.

You should never approach an eyrie in such a way that you surprise the eagle and frighten her off at the last moment. If you've to make a hidden approach, see that you give her plenty of warning—talking loudly or making some kind of recognisable noise—so that she can clear the nest while you're still some distance away.

Female buzzard arriving at nest. The buzzard is shy, cunning, and easily frightened at nesting time.

I've watched eagles for days, sometimes weeks, on end, very often from hiding places situated at anything from 8 feet to 80 from an eyrie. But this is something requiring great care, and I don't recommend it unless you're in company with someone who knows what he's about, or have had a lot of experience with other birds.

However, since you may not have a great deal of time, here are a few suggestions based on my own way of working with eagles.

The best way of all is to have a strong, well-camouflaged hiding place in position long before the eagle ever carries a branch or a clump of heather to the eyrie. Your guess about

81

the eyrie to be used may be wrong, but that's a chance you'll have to take.

What you want is a structure that will stand up to strong winds and heavy rains, and won't collapse under a weight of snow. Ideally, a space between two rocks or big boulders is what you want, so that you can lay branches over the top to form a roof. If there are no branches on the spot you'll have to take them, or something like them with you.

The branches are weighted down with stones. Then clumps of heather or moor grass are piled on top. You can make the hide more comfortable by laying a sheet of waterproof material over the branches before you pile on the heather or grass. You can do the same with the front and back of your hide.

Once you've built such a place it's best to forget about it until the eagle has hatched her brood. I never presume too closely on eagles when they've eggs and I think it's the best way.

If you mean to go to the hill yourself you should be at your hide before daylight, unless you've sited it in such a place that you can make a completely hidden approach.

But bear in mind that eagles have good ears, that the hen will fly from the nest as readily during darkness as she will during the day, and that once she's in the air she's going to see you if you're seeable. Once that happens you might as well go home. This is one of the reasons why you're better with a hide far back from the vicinity of the nest.

It's far safer to go boldly in daylight with a shepherd or stalker on his rounds. Once you're in your hide the eagle's attention will be occupied by the man who leaves. He can either let you out on his return journey, or you can leave by yourself so long as you can do so without the eagle knowing about it. The best thing is always to treat eagle-watching as a job for two.

There's really no point in working closer than 300 or 400 yards from an eyrie unless you've some special purpose in mind, and there's certainly no need to go closer than 100 yards unless you're aiming to take photographs or films. If this is what you have in mind, remember that this is a specialist technique which shouldn't be attempted without consulting an experienced worker who can point out all the dangers and pitfalls. There's absolutely no excuse for upsetting an eagle in the slightest degree.

If your eyrie contains eggs when you find it, you should postpone the erection of any kind of hiding place closer than 400 yards until after the young have hatched.

If the eyrie already contains eaglets you can begin work right away. But you shouldn't complete your hide right away, unless it's well back from the nest (over 200 yards), and unless you can do it quickly, in such a way that there's nothing new for the eagle to see. A new heap of heather or a new arrangement of stones won't upset her ; she won't even notice. But an alien object will—an object like a great tent of hessian stuck openly on a bare hill.

So bear in mind that any strange erection within a few hundred yards of the eyrie is going to keep the eagle off until she's satisfied it's harmless. What you're trying to do is overcome the disadvantages of wide open country and a bird that can command a view of the whole parish. You won't solve the problem by doing a disappearing act into a brand new hide and leaving the eagle to worry about where you've gone.

Your constant aim, therefore, is to have a hiding place at a point of vantage without the eagles being aware that anything new has been added to the landscape as they knew it.

Provided you take all these precautions, eagles aren't difficult to get along with. And once you've gone to all this trouble to see eagles at short range there are certain things you might as well do to get the maximum benefit from your work.

You can collect all pellets, and make a note of all prey on the nest. If you can get into the nest you should mark all prey in such a way that you won't include it again on your list at your next visit, if it's still lying unused. Breaking a leg of each item is as good a way as any.

While you're doing all these things you'll be able to note that eagles don't attack human beings at the nest, and don't stay around screaming at you. You'll also note that eaglets are as harmless as barn-door chicks.

While you're on the hill you should keep constant lookout for the hunting eagle. He's easy enough to see when he's flying above the skyline ; when he's below it, flying along a hillside, he isn't.

Watch any eagle you see near lambs in spring, and note if he makes any attempt to molest them. How do the ewes behave when the eagle's about ?

Lastly, a word of warning. If you're taking a small terrier to the hill with you at this time, see that the dog doesn't get too far ahead of you or out of sight for long, because some eagles will attack terriers and some have killed them. The assumption is that they mistake the dog for a fox, but that will be little consolation to the terrier, or to you.

You can always look for the buzzard on eagle ground, because their requirements are much the same. Buzzards nest in trees or rocks, and a crag which attracts an eagle will also attract a buzzard, as well as peregrine falcon or kestrel. When searching cliffs or crags you should bear in mind all these possibilities.

It isn't unusual to find two or more of these birds of prey nesting in close proximity. You may find them within 200 yards of each other. I've had eagle and peregrine 100 yards apart, peregrine and buzzard 100 yards apart, and all

three on the same hillside within 500 yards.

This kind of association is well worth watching. If there's a pair of ravens in the neighbourhood you'll be sure to see plenty of action because these birds spend a great deal of their time harrying golden eagles.

When you're watching these birds you'll notice that the reaction of the different species is different. The eagle will come off the nest quietly and very soon pass out of sight ; the buzzard will mount and circle, mewing for a time, then gradually drift away ; the peregrine will fly round your head screaming abuse ; the raven will probably be stealthily away before you reach the spot.

A vantage point from which you can watch such a community should be looked for at once. Here you have a wonderful opportunity of seeing something of the tolerance of birds of prey towards each other at this time. You'll also see what happens when one trespasses on the territory of another.

Eagle will drive off falcon, and falcon will pitch into eagle, when one flies through the other's " air space." Even the little kestrel will

assault the mighty eagle. The raven will frequently harry the eagle, anywhere, at any time, without any trespass having been committed.

Buzzards, it's generally agreed by those who have studied them closely, are shy and cunning if you try to make their too close acquaintance. But they'll tolerate you at a reasonable distance, so you should aim at watching from a distance of 100 yards or so.

With a good hide, you can get quickly to grips with the peregrine falcon, especially if you build it of local materials —stones, boulders, heather, bracken.

There's been a lot of argument about whether the buzzard has any sense of smell. The way some of them behave when a human being is hidden near the nest, upwind, often makes me wonder. I've noticed striking changes in buzzard behaviour with a change of wind.

The kestrel is a relatively easy subject at close quarters. At a distance of 200 yards you'll be ignored so long as you sit quietly, even although you're unconcealed. If you want in closer than that you'll need some kind of hide. But you can't walk in and out of a hide in full view of the birds and expect them to carry on as though you didn't exist. You'll need someone with you to hold their attention when you're going in or coming out.

The sparrowhawk used to be common; now it is scarce in many parts of the country. It is now protected by law, like all our other birds of prey, but it is still shot by many people at every opportunity. This is due mainly to the fact that it kills song birds and game chicks, although there's no evidence

(Opposite, above) *Cock Montagu's harrier feeding twin chicks in the nest on a grouse moor. This very rare hawk was photographed in Scotland, where it nested for the first time in 1953.*

(Opposite, below) *Female kestrel brooding chicks on a rock ledge in deer forest.*

at all that it makes any impact on the numbers of either. Predators seldom affect the numbers of their prey species.

The way things are going it's likely that the sparrowhawk will disappear altogether from many parts of the country. It may even become an uncommon bird, as the merlin already is.

This bold, dashing hawk—sharp-faced, needle-beaked, yellow-taloned, with eyes like jewels—is an easy subject for the watcher. Just as it's an easy target for the shooter. In the breeding season you can work close to it without upsetting it.

It builds its nest in a tall tree, usually near the main stem. Nearby the cock has his " plucking stool "—the place to which he carries prey for plucking before he takes it to the nest. You can have a hide near the plucking stool, and one up beside the nest if you like. If you build both carefully you'll have no trouble with the birds.

Make a point of studying the sparrowhawk at nesting time. What are the birds killing? Is the hen killing woodpigeons? How many small birds are killed during the nesting period?

As we've seen, birds of prey that nest on rocks or crags, or even in trees, can be watched from a distance with the aid of telescope or binoculars. You're faced with quite a different problem when your bird is nesting in thick ground cover, as the merlin and harriers do.

You can watch, from a distance, the comings and goings of the birds. You can do it with binoculars, and you can do it without a hide so long as you're inconspicuous. But

(Opposite, above) *Female sparrowhawk with well-grown young a* *their nest in a larch tree—a typical nesting site*

(Opposite, below) *Female kestrel at nest in Scots pine. When th* *kestrel breeds in trees she uses the old nest of crow, magpie o* *sparrowhawk*

the country favoured by these birds is usually open, so if you want to get in closer you'll need cover of some kind.

From a hiding place, say at 100 yards from a nest, you'll see the birds working about. You'll see the jack merlin flying in with prey, and perhaps the harrier passing prey to his mate in the air ; but you'll see nothing of what goes on down in the heather once the female has returned to the nest. You can watch the growth of the young, or note the prey being killed, simply by making regular visits to the nest. But if you want to see the hen brooding her young, and feeding them, you'll have to move close in.

Fortunately, this isn't very difficult, so long as you take proper precautions. Of course, it's always better to make your first attempt in the company of an experienced person. But let us assume you've to start on your own.

Harriers and merlins frequently nest on grouse moors, and on grouse moors there are usually shooting butts. If the nest is near a butt your problem is solved from the beginning. You make use of the butt. Cover it over so that you'll be hidden from above, and get inside.

If the nest isn't near a butt, you'll have to bring one, or something like one, to the spot you've chosen.

To do this you build a new butt—no bigger than you require for sitting in—a hundred yards, or a bit more, from the nest. You can build it complete, so long as you work quickly, using four strong posts, wire netting, heather, grass and peat, or whatever the local material is. Make it look like the real thing and the birds will ignore it. And do your building late in the daytime.

Leave your butt in position for a day. On the second, third and fourth day you can move it closer by stages, twenty yards or so at a time, either moving it bodily or stripping it and reassembling it at each move. The final distance will be about 10 yards. This may strike you as tedious work, but

it's essential. You
don't want scarey birds
on your hands; you want
them to behave naturally, treating
your hide as part of the landscape. If
you're not prepared to take this trouble you
should leave the birds alone. Furthermore, if
you are impatient, or are not prepared to sit quietly
for lengthy periods, you would be better to leave all birds
of prey alone.

Remember, once your hide is in its final position, you'll
need someone with you—someone the birds can watch leaving
after you've been put in, and someone they can watch arriving
to let you out. It's worse than useless, and grossly unfair
to the birds, to try to cut corners in this business of hides.
There are no short-cuts.

Many people take the view that it's unfair to pry into bird
affairs because the birds may be frightened or upset. The
point is admissible, and the criticism very often true. But
if you proceed carefully, there should be no upset to the
birds, and you should always be prepared to pack up at
once when you meet a pair who don't take kindly to what
you're doing.

On the high tops, over 3,000 feet, you'll find the ptarmigan
—the grouse who lives on the roof of the world. It's the

only member of the family, indeed the only British bird, that turns white in winter.

Raven

It takes really severe weather—blizzards or blanketing snow—to drive the ptarmigan to the low ground. He's the last to leave the high ground, so normally you've to seek him on the tops, whether to look at him or shoot him.

Ptarmigan nest on high, boulder-strewn flats, and finding a hen on eggs is a matter of cold searching. She sits closely, until almost trodden upon, and you may, literally, step over her without flushing her.

Carrion Crow

If you wish to keep track of a nest for later visits, you'd be well advised to mark the place, for a sitting ptarmigan can be as hard to find a second time as the first. The simplest way is to erect a small, but obvious, cairn near the nest. It won't worry the birds and will make things easy for you.

Jay

On the lower slopes and heather moors, where the red grouse is found, you can mark nests by placing two or three stones, one on top of another, a few yards away.

Jackdaw

Grouse, like ptarmigan, sit close, and may not move even when you're

(Opposite, above)
Hen partridge settling on nest containing 16 eggs. This nest was in woodland, in a thick stand of nettles.

(Opposite, below)
Hen capercaillie bringing off chicks in Forestry Commission plantation in Scotland.

Rook

standing over them. Finding nests is therefore a matter of hard searching on every likely area of heather, which is a slow business.

If you're anxious to find all the nests on a given area you'll find a steady, well-disciplined Labrador retriever or pointer a great help. Dogging for nests proved satisfactory in Angus where the inquiry into the decline of the red grouse was carried on for some years.

Another way of finding nests is to lash the heather with rope. A 60 feet length of rope, with one person at either end, is drawn over the heather. As the taut rope travels, the heather bends forward then springs upright again. This flushes a lot of grouse, but not all of them.

During the nesting season grouse aren't difficult subjects to watch. On ground where they're left in peace they're easy. By quietly pottering about you'll see hens with broods, grouse feeding, eating grit, dust-bathing and even drinking. Despite all that has been said to the contrary, grouse do drink water.

If you find a dead grouse, which obviously hasn't died by violence, you should hand it over to the keeper or moor owner. Grouse are important game birds, subject to certain diseases, and moor owners like to know if there's disease on their ground.

Make a note of deaths by predators. What predators are killing grouse? And how many grouse? What birds are stealing eggs? Look in the nests of winged predators, and at the dens of ground predators like the fox to see if they're taking grouse. Trying to establish the relationships in such a community is interesting work. It's been established that predation makes little difference to grouse numbers, so don't begin taking sides in predator-prey relationships.

One thing you must do—obtain the permission of the moor owner to go looking for grouse. This is common courtesy.

Some owners are sticky, but most will co-operate when they realise you're really interested in grouse and other moorland birds, and are a dependable person.

On lower moors you'll quite often find partridges nesting beside the red grouse in the heather. It isn't true of all areas, but it is of many, especially where the heather is close to arable land.

One of the great discoveries of recent years has been that many animal populations are self-regulatory. Dr. Jenkins, and his fellow workers, have shown that the red grouse regulates its numbers to suit the carrying capacity of the moor, and that predation is an insignificant factor.

The grouse do not, of course, sit down and make a decision about this. Responding to the influences of the environment, the supply and quality of heather among them, the cock grouse take over a sufficient territory and hold it against competitors by aggressive display.

The strongest grouse hold the territories, and when all available territories have been taken, the surplus birds have to leave, or live from hand to mouth, or die. They are really surplus to the carrying capacity of the ground, and it makes little difference how they die after they have left it, or whether they find new ground elsewhere. The old moor has lost them anyway.

Thus it is easily seen that the presence of predators on a grouse moor is natural and inevitable, even necessary. The numbers of predators do not determine the number of grouse; it is more nearly the other way round.

The old-fashioned practice of killing predators as routine is therefore a mistaken one.

The main red grouse research to-day is in the hands of the Nature Conservancy's Unit of Grouse and Moorland Ecology, working from Aberdeen University. Dr Adam Watson is now in charge of this team.

The partridge is an interesting bird to work with, and if you go about your work quietly, and gently, it can also be very easy. The display of birds when still in covey, and that of mated males and hens in the spring, are easy enough to watch because they take place in the open. All you need is a hiding place and a pair of field glasses.

The nesting partridge is far more secretive and, understandably, owners of ground don't usually like people trying to probe too deeply into the secret. But there's always the nest somewhere that you can keep your eye on, without treading on anyone's toes.

Partridges like to nest in hedge-bottoms, at the bottom of old dry-stone walls, in tangled ditches, and in clumps of vegetation, including nettles.

When the hen begins her nest the cover is usually scant, and you might think her careless in selecting such a poor screen. But, while she is laying, she covers her eggs with grass and leaves after each visit, and by the time she is ready to sit the cover is usually well above her head, and thick. Most sitting partridges are invisible.

Most sitting partridges stay down tight, and most will flush only when almost trodden upon. But birds vary. Some take fright readily early on in the incubation period; others will allow themselves to be stroked on the nest, a practice not generally recommended. It is best not to visit your partridge until she is well down on her eggs.

At this time you can watch the hen going off to feed, and being escorted back to the nest by the cock. If she is the quiet, close type you can try and be with her at hatching time, and see how she passes the first-hatched chicks over to the cock, who will be in attendance.

When the hatch is complete both birds lead the chicks away, tending and brooding their quota. The cock will try to rear the brood if his hen is killed.

Carrion crow with fully-fledged young at nest in Scots pine.

With members of the crow family, you'll find that baiting is a useful technique outside the breeding season. I use it a great deal. Baiting means laying down food at a place of your choosing to persuade the birds to come there, or maintaining a supply of food at a spot the birds are already visiting because they've found food there in the past.

For example, if you find ravens or hoodie crows feeding on a dead sheep or deer, you can keep them coming to the spot by maintaining the food supply. This presupposes, of course, that the place is an easy one to watch. In most cases, it's better to start from scratch at a place of your own choice.

After making a suitable hiding place you lay down food

that will attract the species you want. You'll get others, but you should aim for the ones you're most concerned with.

On deer forest, a dead deer or sheep will attract ravens and others. On a winter morning you may find three or four foxes round such a carcase, or half a dozen ravens accompanied by an eagle or a buzzard. You never know exactly what you're going to find, and you'll see all sorts of arguments. You'll find that there's a "peck order" among these scavengers, as there is among poultry.

You can bait for carrion crows and magpies near home, even in your garden. I've found that an egg a day brings the magpies my way. I put out one each evening and watch the magpies in the morning. And, of course, I anchor the egg so that a bird can't fly off with it.

A lump of fat, or a marrow bone, fastened to the trunk of a tree will attract crows, magpies, jackdaws and rooks, and individual birds will spend minutes at a time stabbing at

A meal of eggs for the jay. This species is a confirmed nest robber.

such a bait. A dead rabbit or hare staked to the ground will bring the shyest crow right up to your hiding-place. But remember, all these birds are extremely wary and easily frightened.

Baiting, as you see, is quite a different thing from watching birds at their nests. The crow family, as a whole, is as shy and scary during the nesting season as at any other time. The rook and the jackdaw are probably the easiest to work with.

Ravens nest early in the year, so you've to seek their nests when the weather is still severe. Whether your raven is living on deer forest, or on the coast, or on inland crags, the approach is the same.

The raven is a bright, intelligent bird—wary and suspicious —and you can't take any liberties. The same applies to the hoodie crow. So if you hope to see much of either bird you'll have to be most cautious. It's always best to leave both alone until they have young at least a week old.

Both birds can be watched from a camouflaged hide a little distance away—say fifty yards. The construction of such a hide should be carried out in easy stages, and the work done late in the day. At all stages the camouflage should be as good as you can make it, using the local materials—birch branches, rowan branches, heather, bracken, or whatever it happens to be.

The hoodie crow is one of the wariest and most cunning of birds and you should never make the mistake of thinking that anything will do. You'll need a good hide, and you'll have to sit perfectly still, or the bird will soon discover the truth. With every man's hand against it, the hoodie is constantly on the alert for danger.

Hoodies can also be watched when they're foraging on the shore. A day or two on the ground will show you where they're working. All you need then is a hiding-place above high-water mark. From it you can watch the birds hunting the tideline, or searching for the eggs of oystercatcher, ringed plover, or duck, or other birds nesting along the shore. And you won't be confined to watching hoodies. There'll be all the shore-nesting birds, and you can observe their reactions to the approach of a marauder like the hoodie.

Magpies, jays, jackdaws and carrion crows are members of the same bright family, and have to be approached with care. Jackdaws in an old building are easy enough subjects, because you can rearrange the scenery without upsetting them. Birds in trees are a different problem entirely.

Rooks present little problem except the physical one of getting up beside them. If you live near a rookery you can watch them simply by sitting down and looking up. If the rookery is near your house, you may be able to see all you want to see from an upstairs window.

Sooner or later, however, you'll probably want to get up beside the birds. The rook has that kind of appeal. This requires a lot of work, but it's work you can spread over a long period. A rookery being an established place, you know your rooks will be back, so you can make your preparations in the off season when there are no birds about and take all the time you want. You can, indeed, build a kind of permanent watch-tower.

What you want is a covered seat in a tall tree, sited so that you have nests all around you and a few close at hand at eye level. Old beech trees are ideal for this, because of their wide-spreading tough branches. But ash, elm and horse-chestnut are also good.

You'll want a platform about 3 feet square, unless you feel you can do with a smaller one.

For the platform use a framework of 2 x 2 inch white pine. Nail and tie them to branches, and nail them together. Stack rope is excellent for tying. The floor should be of wood

Pylon hide 25 feet high, built for studying and photographing carrion crows at the nest. Erecting a pylon of this strength and height is work for several pairs of hands and has to be done piecemeal so as not to alarm the crows.

The grey-white parchment face of the rook, the feature which most readily distinguishes it from the carrion crow.

$\frac{5}{8}$ of an inch thick, and tacked down with 2-inch nails. A seat like this is easily made. You may have to cut a few small branches out of the way, so take a saw with you. And use a ladder for getting up to the easy climbing.

Now you need some cover. For this you require a framework. Use 2 x 1 inch uprights, about 4 feet long, one fastened to each of the four corners of your platform. Tie the tops to overhead branches, or otherwise secure them, so that they'll be vertical and rigid. Then nail cross-pieces of the same thickness along the top, from corner to corner, and your framework is complete.

(Opposite) *Rooks flying into their nests in the month of Marc, Traditionally, the 1st of March is the beginning of the rooks' breedir, seaso.*

Jackdaw with food pouch loaded arriving at nest in hollow tree.

You can cover the whole thing over with wire netting and hessian, or wire netting and waterproof material ; or you can box it in with wood if you want a permanent hide and wood is no problem. You don't need netting if you're boxing up. The netting is to prevent the hessian or other material from flapping in the wind.

Now your hide is in position, and when the rooks begin building their nests in March they'll take no notice of it. More likely, many of them will use it as a perch. There is endless pleasure and instruction to be derived from sitting aloft with the rooks in March and April, and in May, and you'll find that the time spent in getting there was worthwhile.

Carrion crows and magpies, which also nest in trees, present quite a different problem.

In the first place you don't know where they're going to nest until they've nested. In the second place both are prone to desert, with very little prodding, until their young are fairly well grown. So you should forget about making the close acquaintance of either until they've nestlings at least a week old.

Because the magpie builds a great thorny ball of a nest there's nothing to be seen once the bird goes inside, so there's little point in making any kind of hiding-place near at hand.

Blue tit

t tit

Coal tit

Long-tailed tit

Willow tit

Early in the mornings, just after daylight, you should look out for crows or magpies which are visiting farmyards. If they are, you should make a point of being there before them on a few mornings to see what they're doing. You can hide in any outbuilding.

Crows and magpies like eggs. Farm hens often lay in holes in corn stacks and the raiders may be stealing these. Or robbing some ground nest where a hen is laying away. Or killing chicks or ducklings. Or mousing among the stacks. Or eating corn. Or assaulting farm kittens. Or feeding on a pig's back. You can learn a lot about crow behaviour by watching them at farms.

You can also learn a lot about the crow family by keeping one of them as a pet. Ravens are protected by law, so you can't take one without a permit. But rooks, jays, jackdaws, magpies and crows aren't protected, so you can take one of them so long as you know how to rear it. In any case, there's usually a youngster available from a shot-up nest, or whose parents have been killed.

As a general rule, taking any wild creature for the specific purpose of making a pet of it is not to be recommended, and you shouldn't do it. But every year there are plenty of surplus, orphaned or unwanted crows of one kind or another to justify breaking this rule.

Provided you live in a house where you've no near neighbours, keeping one of these birds presents little problem. You'll learn a lot about the particular species.

A great advantage of having one of these birds tame is that you can study its hunting methods and its food. Mind you, if you keep hens, you'll have a bit of trouble teaching it to leave eggs and chicks alone.

You should encourage your bird to fend for itself as soon as it's able to do so. Note what kind of insect food it takes, and how it behaves when you turn over a stone or tear a rotten tree stump apart. Observe how it behaves towards dogs and cats ; its reaction to the presence of a hedgehog, a frog, a toad, a sexton beetle. And note any food preferences. How do crows and magpies treat slugs and earthworms ? Do they hide food ? And, if so, do they remember where they have hidden it ?

With a bird of this kind, free moving and at the same time under control, the possibilities are endless.

Visitors to the bird table :
(Above) *Hen pheasant.*
(Below) *Roebuck.*

The most obvious way to begin studying members of the tit family is to feed them in winter—not just by throwing out food in a haphazard manner, but by planning your feeding arrangements.

First of all you want a bird table. This needn't be elaborate, but it should be secure. It can be placed in any position that suits your convenience—near a window, for example, so that you can watch from inside on cold winter days—but it should also give the birds a clear view of any approaching cat. Keeping a bird table going is just another form of baiting, and the birds will come almost anywhere you want them to.

The easiest of tables to make consists of an upright of 2 x 2 inch red pine, firmly stuck in the ground, and reaching a height of 4 feet or so. The top should be about 18 inches square, and it should have a lip round the edge to prevent food from spilling off. A gutter at each corner is also advisable, as it lets rain run off quickly.

Of course, you can put a roof over the table. And you can close it on the weather side. You can even put it on a swivel so that it will always turn in the wind and have the open side away from the weather.

Near the table, above it or alongside, but placed higher, there should be a length of stout string from which you can suspend pieces of fat, a half coconut, a peanut dispenser, or a tit bell, or anything that takes your fancy as a feeding gadget. There are many feeding gadgets on the market to-day, but you can make them all yourself if you like—and if you're handy.

Once your bird table is up you should, of course, cater for as many birds as you can. Household scraps, brown bread, grain, seeds, raisins and fat will attract thrushes, blackbirds, robins, dunnocks, finches and others. You can, if you like, put up a seed hopper for the finches. A pudding made of wholewheat bread, fruit and fat will appeal to most of the birds and it's excellent winter food. The shortest way to a robin's confidence is to provide him with meal worms.

For the tits you'll have peanuts (shelled and unsalted) in your dispenser. In the bell or coconut you can have fat or a mixture of nuts and fat. From the string you can hang fat, a marrow bone, cooked bones and chickens' keels.

If you want to attract still other birds you can cater accordingly. A marrow bone tied to a handy tree, or to the upright of the bird table, will soon be found by the great spotted woodpecker if there's one about. Grain laid out in a few likely places will bring woodpigeons, pheasants, waterhens, ducks, jays, or squirrels, depending on where you live.

The bird table illustrated here has attracted pheasant,

Three species of tit, blue tit, coal tit and great tit, come to feed on the peanut dispenser.

(Above) *Chaffinch at bird table after snowfall.*
(Below) *The great tit is also puzzled by the snow.*

(Above, left) *Great spotted woodpecker at nut dispenser.* (Above, right) *Cock sparrow at nesting box designed for tits.* (Below) *Blackbird, woodpigeons and water-hen feeding under the bird table.*

Great tit perched at kitchen window waiting for the nut dispenser to be replenished.

carrion crow, woodpigeons, woodpecker, jackdaw, water-hen, dunnock, yellowhammer, chaffinch, greenfinch, robin, thrush, blackbird, starling, sparrow, blue tit, coal tit, great tit, a grey squirrel, and a roebuck.

In addition to putting out food in winter, you should put up nesting boxes for the tits. They should be fixed to a tree trunk, or a wall, in your garden or in nearby woodland. Have the boxes with hinged lids, so that you can look in once in a while. Place them at a height to suit your convenience, so long as there are no cats about ; site them higher if cats are likely to be a bother. Most of my boxes are about 9 feet from the ground.

Boxes should be made of rough wood, about $\frac{3}{4}$ inch thick. They should be put up at the beginning of the winter, to allow them to weather, and so that the birds can become used to them before the spring. Creosote them before putting them out, and yearly in autumn after that—not in spring.

You can face the boxes pretty well as you like, but you should avoid a southern exposure unless the box is shaded, and a western exposure unless there's protection from the rain. South-east or south-west exposures are best as a general rule.

Tit boxes should be about $4\frac{1}{2}$ inches square and should have the roof projecting on sides and front to shed water. Depth at front should be 8 inches. At the back it should be 10 inches. This gives a roof sloping to the front. The entrance hole should be placed high in the front—about 2 inches from the top—as tits like a drop down inside. It should be $1\frac{1}{8}$ inches in diameter; certainly not more than $1\frac{1}{4}$ inches. The floor shouldn't be tacked on to the bottom; it should be set in so that there's no exposed joint for water to seep through. Don't nail the box directly to tree trunk or wall, as it becomes wet at the back with rain running down. Fix it to a strap of wood first, and nail the strap to the tree above and below the nesting box.

Boxes for birds like nuthatches follow the same pattern, but they should be bigger—about double the height, about 6 inches square, and with a hole 2 inches in diameter. For robins and flycatchers they can be about 4 x 4 inches square, and about 8 inches deep. The front should be closed a little less than half-way up the remainder being left open.

Each species has its special requirements in the way of elbow room, so don't place your boxes too near each other. Spread them out. And have them in places you can get to without crashing through thick cover or becoming entangled in low-spreading branches. Put them in trees with some clear way round them.

Garden birds are usually easy to watch; they wouldn't be in the garden if they didn't have a high tolerance of human beings. Most of them can be studied at close quarters without any special preparation, and they'll feed their young, and go about their affairs, while you're seated a few yards away, so long as you sit still. Many, like robins, flycatchers, starlings, tits and nuthatches, will use nesting boxes provided for them.

Depending on where you live, and the size and nature of your garden, you may have anything from half a dozen to a score of species nesting with you ; so you can learn a lot about birds without leaving home.

You can encourage birds to nest by letting parts of the garden go " wild " and by planting a variety of shrubs or fruit bushes. You can create thickets by piling hedge clippings in a corner and letting the grass grow through them : these will attract birds like willow warblers, dunnocks and whitethroats.

You'll be surprised, if you put out the combings from your dog's coat, and a few handfuls of small feathers from an old feather duster, how quickly the birds will make use of them in the nesting season.

If you become seriously interested in a species—say the blackbirds, or thrushes, or great tits in your garden and round about—and want to be able to identify individuals on sight, you might consider colour ringing. The rings are readily available ; the know-how isn't. So, before you attempt to catch up a bird, let alone ring it, do take expert advice.

If you're at school, consult your science master. Join a Natural History Society. Get an expert to teach you. Read up the subject; there are many fine books available. But don't touch the birds until you know what you're doing.

Outside your garden, there's a lot you can do apart from going the rounds with binoculars as often as you can. This is true of any season of the year. Perhaps I can best illustrate what I mean by describing some of my own methods of approaching birds near my home.

I've often used a big cornstack in the corner of a field as a winter observation post. When I had a morning to spare I used to go there and sit under the trestle from dawn until a few hours after. Woodpigeons and pheasants, fieldfares, reed buntings, finches, magpies, gulls, crows and jackdaws used to work close to the stacks looking for food. The field was a great one for bird flocks, and sometimes there would be golden plovers as well.

On many mornings I scattered a few handfuls of grain, and other food, near the stacks, to encourage the birds to come close in.

Many of the birds kept coming right through to the spring

threshing, and I've watched, from my chosen stack, the display of woodpigeons, pheasants, rooks and crows, within 25 feet.

I've seen a weasel stalk a peewit that was wet after a bath, then miss it because a magpie yattered a warning. I've seen two magpies assaulting a small rabbit. I've watched a hen sparrowhawk strike down a woodpigeon, and ride it to earth in a cloud of feathers. And I've seen a fox slinking up the inside of the dry-stone wall, along the woodside, to lie in ambush for the pheasants when they eventually sprinted to cover.

That I had chosen a good observation post was proved when, one morning, I disturbed a fox from my seat under the trestle. Clearly, he had weighed up the possibilities of the place as an ambush.

In another field, on the edge of the wood, I used to build a hiding-place of wire netting and cover it with straw sheaves from the threshing. When these were all tied in place I had a good hide and a warm one. Birds used to sit on it.

From it I've watched, at different times, fieldfares, redwings, waxwings and golden plovers ; grey geese once pitched close to it ; crows, jackdaws, magpies, peewits, golden plovers, larks, ducks, gulls, partridges and moorhens have fed close to it. Pheasants have preened in its shelter. And once a roe deer came and nibbled before he could own my scent.

Then there was the pond. I had a hiding-place there for a long time, and I used it at all seasons, but mostly at nesting time. From it I've watched, at the same time, a moorhen with her brood paddling behind her, a mallard on eggs and a reed bunting feeding young. I've watched the sedge warbler there, and seen a toad climbing into a nest beside a sitting moorhen.

The bigger the pond the more there usually is to see, and

(Opposite) *Swans and mallards during a mid-winter freeze up*

with a hiding-place on the water's edge, one can watch, in comfort, such birds as coots, grebes, dabchicks, herons, mallards, moorhens and reed buntings at any time of the year.

None of these things involved me in much work, or cost me any extra time. And instead of sitting around in these places, exposed to the weather, and trying hard not to be seen, I could sit in comfort, with the assurance that I couldn't be seen by any eyes.

Another place I used to hide in was a pullet house in my stackyard. I went there early in the morning and I've had a covey of partridges feeding, preening and dozing within ten feet of my nose. I've had a magpie draining an egg three feet from the toe of my boot. And I've watched a tawny owl mousing in broad daylight, and swooping at one of my cats.

Of course, none of this is easy to do away from home, so one falls back on the routine method of taking convenient natural cover and watching through glasses. But when I've been settled in one place for a few days I've often taken the trouble to rig up some kind of hiding-place near any spot where birds were flocking.

For example, where waders are flocking close to your home in winter, or if you can reach them quickly, a prepared hiding-place will more than justify the trouble of erecting it. Apart from the shelter it gives on cold, wet, or blustery mornings, it puts you right in the middle of the flock.

I find it more satisfying to view such shy, wary birds at 20 feet rather than 150 yards. There's no particular virtue in lying back 150 yards if you can view in comfort, and more clearly, from a fraction of the distance.

Furthermore, since many waders are difficult to identify, the closer you are the more accurate you can be in your description of a bird you might want to identify later on.

In autumn and winter, waders of many kinds will be found

Winter visitors :
    (Above, left) *Fieldfare.* (Above, right) *Redwing.*
    (Below, left) *Waxwing.* (Below, right) *Whooper swan.*

on estuaries and coastal mudflats, as well as at inland reservoirs and sewage farms. If you live handy to any such places a permanent hide is an advantage. Shooting men build hides, and use decoys, for wildfowl and woodpigeons, and there's no reason why you shouldn't do the same.

Any time you meet a strange bird, or one about which you aren't sure, you should note down, immediately, such things as its size, shape, markings, colour of beak and legs, the exact zones of plumage colour, the distance the bird was from you, the time of year, the time of day, and the direction of the light.

With these things written down you can check your description against the standard. Don't be satisfied with looking at the bird then looking at a set of coloured drawings ; that way you'll almost certainly find the bird you want to find rather than the one you saw.

Don't worry about making mistakes in identity. Everybody makes mistakes. Anyone who says he hasn't, just hasn't admitted it to himself.

And don't be worried if you make a long series of observations on a bird, then find it isn't the bird you thought it was. You've got your observations. All you've to change is the bird's name. That's better than having a long list of birds seen, and nothing at all recorded about what you've seen them doing.

In the breeding season, birds of the wader group aren't so

easily approached. In the first place you don't have the concentrations ; secondly, they usually nest where there's little cover ; thirdly, most of them are shy and wary.

But let me explain how I approach some of the common ones that you can see easily for yourself : the curlew, peewit, snipe and oystercatcher.

If I'm watching from a distance, using field glasses, I choose a position (if possible) between the birds and the sun. That way I have front lighting on the birds, and I have the sun at my back while the birds have it in their eyes. This is even more so in the early morning and in the evening when the sun is low.

I choose a tree, or a hedge, or a peat hummock to sit against, so that my outline is lost ; if there's no cover at all I make some with whatever is lying to hand—reeds, rushes, grass, sods, peat, heather or stones.

If I want to get closer, and I usually do, I make a proper hide and sit it in the middle of the ground. A hide put up in a field where several peewits are nesting won't annoy the birds. Nor will one 25 yards or so from a curlew's nest annoy the curlews.

Where I have a snipe in dense rushes I put up a screen

Philip Rickman

Sand martin at nesting burrow in sand-pit.

of netting and tie bundles of rushes to it ; later I box it in behind, and stand rushes all round. The snipe takes no notice. And now I can watch her until the time she leads her chicks from the nest.

I do the same with oystercatchers as I do with curlews and peewits. With sandpipers I do the same. And with golden plovers.

For birds like grebes or coots, or the bittern if you're in bittern country, you might want a rough raft, housed in with netting and rushes, and anchored where it gives a view of the birds and their nest. Where you use entirely local growth, in this fashion, there's little risk of upset to the birds.

Many small birds can be watched as easily as the birds in your garden, if they're nesting where you can have a view from thirty feet or so away.

In this context are birds like willow warblers, nightingales, dippers, wagtails, flycatchers, tits, woodpeckers, pipits, yellowhammers, linnets and dunnocks.   You can watch swallows from inside the building where they're nesting, and you can use a light to help you.

For watching swallows you need nothing more than something to sit on, because the birds will come and go with you close at hand.   But, if you're studying the swallows on your own premises, where they're always round your ears, as it were, you can learn a lot from marking them in some way so that you can recognise individuals.

When I lived in a farmhouse I put coloured rings on the legs of my swallows.   In this way I found out that one hen had made the journey to Africa and back five times before I had to move elsewhere.   I don't know what happened to her after that, but I have no doubt at all that she would keep

Swallow arrives at nest in the roof of a barn.

coming back to the same place for the rest of her life.

A neighbour of mine, a farmer with a great interest in birds, was able to recognise one of his swallows because of its mismarked plumage. He discovered that the bird nested on the same rafter, and on the same part of the same rafter, each year. This is true of most swallows.

If you want to look more closely at nesting swallows, by getting up on the rafters beside them, you require some sort of screen between you and the birds. Old hessian pegged from roof to rafters will do fine, and you can then watch the birds from five or six feet distance.

Swallows, house martins and sand martins are all very confiding birds which can be viewed from close at hand without trouble. The house martin, like the swallow, will go about its affairs while you are sitting below the nests. But, if you want to get in close to the sand martins, you require cover of some kind. It doesn't have to be elaborate, but you should wait until the birds are busy feeding chicks in the burrows.

Sand martins make their nesting burrows in sandy river banks, sandpits, and even shale, or blaes, cuttings. The birds dig with their beaks and push the loose material behind them with their feet.

A bird you won't see at the nest unless you can get inside, and close, is the swift. And the swift is worth watching. If you can get a view of the nest from inside the building, all you need in the way of cover is a barricade between you and the nest—a sheet of hardboard, a bit of an old door, or a sheet of black cloth. Use a red light—shining down, not on to the nest—and you'll see all there is to see. You can get as close as you like to a swift's nest so long as the bird can't see you.

Among the easiest of birds to watch are colonial nesting seabirds like gannets, puffins, razorbills, guillemots or fulmars.

Fulmar petrel incubating her single egg on a rock ledge.

You can sit right among them and they'll carry on as though you didn't exist. There are many famous breeding stations up and down the country, and you should make a point of spending a day at one of them. You'll have an exciting and full day, and you'll never have birds as close with so little trouble.

Where fulmars are nesting, you can spend a rewarding hour doing nothing more than sitting on a cliff top watching these birds in flight. They're unsurpassed masters of gliding and drifting, their flight buoyant and effortless even on the stormiest days.

Nesting fulmars, incubating their single egg on rock shelf or grassy hollow, will sit tight and allow you within a few yards before taking flight. Others will allow you within a

Close-up of a young gannet, recently left the nest.

few feet. But be careful about prying too closely, for the fulmar has the habit of disgorging the oily contents of its crop at an intruder.

Puffins will also allow you in close, in full view, so long as you approach quietly and in stages. You can watch the birds whirring down to the sea, and returning to their stances. These birds nest in burrows or rock pockets, mostly out of sight but sometimes exposed to view. Be careful about thrusting your hand into an occupied burrow; the puffin can nip.

Gannets are easy. You can, literally, sit among them. Their nesting season is long, and July is a good month to

(Opposite) *Great skua, or bonxie, attacking intruder.*

visit a breeding station. Note that the birds have no nostrils ; that they have binocular vision.

Try and be at a station when the young birds, in their plumage of black spotted with white, go down to the sea. Make a point of watching gannets diving for fish. How long can a bird stay under? Does any of them swallow fish on the surface of the water? How far is the fishing ground from the nesting cliff?

Many birds have a restricted distribution, so there will be times when you'll have to travel to see what you want to see. The man who wants to see kites has to go to Wales ; if I want to see avocets, red-legged partridges, or nightingales, I have to go to England ; anyone in England or Wales who wants to see great skuas, or nesting grey geese, or golden eagles, has to travel to some part of Scotland.

The Shetlands are one such special area. There you will find the great skua, the Arctic skua, the whimbrel, the red-throated diver, and other less common birds, sometimes in considerable numbers.

The great skua, known in Shetland as the bonxie, is notable for its attacks on people who invade its nesting grounds. The birds come in to the attack with great boldness, and strike with their feet. Such attacks are disconcerting, and the bird can hit hard, but there is no real danger.

Watching these big skuas isn't difficult. Once their eggs are well incubated they'll put up with almost any kind of hide in the middle of their breeding grounds. The birds will even tolerate you a dozen yards away, without a hide, so long as you get well down, with your head covered against attack, and remain still.

The bonxie is well worth watching away from the nest. It is a predator on the eggs and ducklings of the eider duck ;

it assaults other birds (gannets, gulls, and others) to make them disgorge their catch of fish ; and it kills other birds. Without a great deal of trouble you should be in a position to see bonxies raiding the nests of eiders, oystercatchers, ringed plovers and gulls.

The Arctic skua is also a pirate and a predator. It isn't so persistent or savage in its assaults on human beings, but it does attack intruders on its nesting ground. This species varies a great deal in plumage, and you'll see three main phases : the light, the dark, and the intermediate. The dark birds are sooty brown all over, and appear black when on the wing.

Because it is almost helpless on land, the red-throated diver makes its nest near the water's edge. The nest will be on the fringe of a lochan, or on an islet on a lochan. In either case it will be so placed that the bird can slip from the eggs into the water at the first hint of danger.

The red-throat can be easily watched if you take a little care. A hide of local materials, placed on the opposite shore of a small lochan will give you all the view you need. Then you'll be able to watch the birds and their young on the water. The old birds fish in the sea, and you'll see them flying over, high and fast, with food for their young.

Finding the nests of red-throats is easy. All you have to do is walk round each lochan and count them.

The whimbrel, often called the little curlew, is not a common bird even in Shetland. But you'll find it if you look for it. Approach it as you would a curlew. Do not persit in forcing your attention on a bird that is obviously nervous.

Birds which have only a precarious foothold in Britain— birds like the osprey, the avocet, the black-tailed godwit, the kite—should be left alone, unless you are prepared to watch them as a member of the party guarding the nests.

Red-throated diver at nest in the Hebrides.

Rarities, in fact, are better forgotten about, unless your main aim is notching up records of species seen. From the point of view of interest, excitement, instruction or hobby, you'll do just as well, if not better, with many commoner birds. Even with some of the commonest.

Take the woodpigeon, for example. Here is a bird which is one of the most difficult to shoot (ask any shooting man) and one of the most difficult to photograph (ask any bird photographer). It is shy and wary. It will desert eggs, or even small young, without very much prodding. Yet you can get to grips with it easily enough if you go about it in the right way.

Curlew on nest in hay-field.

You can bring woodpigeons to a bird table by putting down grain round about it, or even on top of it.

You can bring them to you in a field, or lane, by erecting a hide in advance, and scattering grain round about it until the birds have learned to come and look for it. Then you can get into your hide and watch them at a distance of a few feet.

Even the nesting woodpigeon isn't so difficult to watch if you choose nest and time with care. The best time is when the young birds are half grown. The best type of nest is one in a low thorn, say ten feet or so from the ground.

Firstly you should choose a spot, about fifteen yards away, which will give you a good view of the nest. Here you'll

Woodpigeon feeding squeakers by regurgitation on nest in hawthorn hedge.

build your hide, spreading the building over a few days. On the day you're ready to begin watching you should tie back any branches in the thorn which obstruct your view of the nest. Now all you want are the birds.

The best times are early morning and towards evening. At this stage the youngsters won't require brooding during the day, so the old birds will come only to feed, and the hen won't stay on until the last feed of the day. The young are fed early, after a night without food, and late in the day, to prepare them for a night without food.

They'll be fed between these times but the visits of the old birds will be unpredictable. So morning and evening are best for you.

Young woodpigeons feed like any other young pigeons ; they push their beaks down the old bird's throat and the food is regurgitated for them. One adult can feed both chicks at once. Sometimes you'll have both parents on the nest together.

You can move your hide in closer as the days pass. The pigeons will accept such moves readily at this stage. To illustrate the point : the woodpigeon photographs here were taken at a distance of five feet.

Most birds can be watched, at more or less close quarters, if proper care is taken. Some are extremely shy at nesting time, and, therefore, more difficult. This means you have to be extremely cautious in your approach. Buzzards, ravens, golden plovers, woodcocks, some of the ducks, and the grey-lag goose, are among the scarey ones.

Contrary to what you might expect, the elusive corncrake is quite easy to work with, while the water rail is shy. The moorhen can be extremely shy, while the coot is usually the opposite. The gulls are easy ; the crow family is not. So don't treat all birds alike. Go slow and learn fast.

You will have trouble finding a corncrake nowadays. The species has disappeared from much of England and Scotland, and is now found in strength in the north-west of Scotland, the northern and outer Isles, and Ireland.

The reasons usually given for its disappearance from most of the country are the increased mechanisation of agriculture and the earlier cutting of hay, but neither of these factors fully explains it.

The corncrake is often referred to as a ventriloquist, but this is because the bird moves about as it calls. It calls at dusk and during the night. The nest is usually in dry grass or other vegetation, and the birds lay up to ten eggs as a rule. A corncrake with chicks will display aggressively towards a man, and may even peck at your feet.

IMPORTANT NOTE : *It is now an offence to disturb, visit, or photograph the nests of all Schedule 1 birds without a licence from the Natural Environment Research Council (Nature Conservancy). For the birds concerned consult the Protection of Birds Act 1954 and later.*

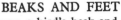

BEAKS AND FEET

In a way, a bird's beak and feet are the tools of its trade. Like any tradesman's tools they tell you how the bird lives and what kind of food it eats.

Some beaks are very obvious pointers. Without being told what the crossbill did for a living you could make a good guess after looking at its crossed pincers, which are for tearing cones. Other obvious beaks are those of the birds of prey—eagles, falcons, hawks and owls —which are for tearing flesh.

The beaks of curlews, woodcocks and snipes are long and slender, for probing soft ground in search of the soil animals on which these birds live. The spatulate beaks of ducks are clearly designed for shovelling, straining and sifting.

If you look at the beak of a hawfinch or a greenfinch, it is obvious that its conical strength is designed for dealing with hard food like the seeds on which the birds live. The soft bill of a nightingale or a robin, on the other hand,

clearly isn't designed for dealing with such food and the birds are, in fact, insect eaters.

The beaks of swallows and nightjars are fly traps. Thrushes and blackbirds have soft bills because they eat insects and worms, but their bills are tough enough to allow them to deal with berries as well.

Heron and kingfisher, despite their great difference in size, have beaks designed for the same kind of work, which is catching fish. You will notice the same type of beak in gannets and divers. The crow family, including the raven, have tough beaks which are jacks of all trades: they can kill, stab, tear and rend.

Feet, like beaks, are a guide to trade. There are webbed feet for swimming, lobed feet for walking on soft surfaces, perching feet as in most small birds, climbing feet as in the case of the woodpeckers, and killing feet as in the case of the eagles, falcons, hawks and owls.

MAMMALS BY NIGHT

THE BADGER

THE BADGER has been called the last of the British bears. In fact, though bear-like in build, he's a true weasel. The bear-like badger ceases to exist as soon as he begins to move. In movement he's all weasel, with the rippling run typical of the whole Mustela clan.

Although stoutly built and usually described as slow, or plodding, he can be as quick off his mark as any weasel. He hasn't the speed to course a full-grown rabbit in the open ; but he's fast enough over a short distance to catch a young one.

Any terrier who has faced a badger knows just how quickly brock can turn his head to bring his jaws into action. A badger rushing on a terrier can move with disconcerting, and demoralising, speed. If you startle a badger in the open, near his den, you'll be astonished at his powers of acceleration.

It's strange that this beast, one of the cleanest of mammals, should so often have the epithet dirty applied to him. When you come to study badgers, however casually, you'll soon realise that the description is a libel.

On the other hand, it would be wrong to think that badgers are completely free of parasites. The sporting newspaper which, many years ago, offered a substantial sum to the man who could produce a genuine badger flea, would quickly lose its money to-day, because badgers do have fleas, and the first thing brock usually does when he leaves his den at night is to give himself a good scratching.

Of course, a flealess animal will scratch. And badgers scratch for reasons not connected with fleas. But badgers

do have fleas, although they aren't anything like so parasite-prone as the fox.

The badger's reputation for cleanliness arises from his house-keeping and his personal habits. He is meticulously clean in himself. And he keeps his den clean. He doesn't foul it up with prey remains as foxes do, and he changes his bedding from time to time.

Outside the sett, he digs his latrines. As he finishes with one he scrapes earth over it, and digs a new one in its place. The presence of such latrines, in use, is an indication of the presence of badgers in a sett.

To bump into a badger accidentally at night is to catch a glimpse of him without learning very much about him. If you're at all interested in badgers, you'll want to do more than that. Getting to know them better is, fortunately, easier than with the other members of the weasel clan, because brock is permanently tied to a known sett or setts.

The badger's den is called a sett, and a badger sett can be distinguished at once from rabbit burrows, whether they've been worked at by a fox or not. The vixen who enlarges a rabbit burrow as a nursery for her cubs is usually content to enlarge one hole and scrape out just as much sand or earth as is absolutely necessary. The badger, on the other hand, is forever digging, and the results of his labours are plain to see.

A well established sett becomes a system of small quarries and big hummocks ; great mounds of earth sloping into large tunnels which have obviously been excavated by a big animal. You realise just how strong a badger is when you see the size of the rocks he can bring up during his digging, and the way he can push them about.

Having discovered your badger sett you've still to make sure that it's occupied at that moment. The way *not* to do this is to let your terrier into the den. You'd soon discover if there was a badger at home all right, but you might be left with a terrier maimed for life. Keep terriers away from badgers. There are other ways of making sure there's a brock in a den.

You should look around the sett for the badger's latrines. These are usually shallow pits, from 6 to 9 inches across and about 9 inches deep. The presence of droppings in these pits will show that badgers have been using the sett, and if the droppings are fresh it means the badgers are still there.

Well-trodden runways radiating from the den indicate the extent of the traffic along these routes. During a period of lush growth, as in the month of May, well-flattened vegetation along the runways will indicate the presence of several badgers and much activity.

Further search will show trees against which badgers have reared to scratch with their strong, bear-like fore-claws. And, sooner or later, you'll find badger tracks on sand, earth, or dried mud in the vicinity.

Badgers, like the rest of us, sometimes misjudge the time, and a beast is sometimes caught by the daylight when he's still some distance from home. If this happens he may hole up somewhere else for the day—even in another badger sett.

The author placing sticks across the entrance to a badger sett, as described in the text.

So you must never be surprised if, on some nights, no badger emerges from a sett which was occupied the day before.

To make sure which entrance holes are being currently used, or most in use, it's a good plan to stick all of them. This consists of placing sticks over each hole, like prison bars, lightly but firmly fixed. This should be done during the early part of the day. The emerging badger will have to thrust the sticks aside to make his exit, and when you visit the den the following morning you'll know at a glance which holes are being used.

You can do better than that, by ensuring not only that badgers have emerged but that badgers have returned. You can do this by visiting the sett late at night. Where sticks

have been pushed aside you should replace them; then, if they're down in the morning, you'll know your badgers are inside.

Once you've established that there are badgers in a sett, and which holes they're using at the time, your next step is to organise your watching.

As always the safest plan is to get off the ground. In woodland, getting off the ground is easy enough: all you've to do is to build a seat in a convenient tree. But you can't do this on an open hillside. At such a site you'll be grounded, and you'll have to depend entirely on remaining unseen and unsmelt. What you can do, on the hill or in woodland, is build a platform about 6 feet high, on 2 inch by 2 inch battens firmly driven into the ground. You can screen this on the side between you and the badgers. With such an arrangement your scent will usually be carried over the beasts' heads.

In woodland, getting off the ground is especially advisable because the wind has an annoying habit of eddying there, and your scent may be carried by a circuitous route to the noses of the badgers, perhaps even right into the den mouth.

Of course, you don't have to get off the ground in woodland, so long as you can keep strict check on the wind. A strong, directional wind is the easiest to keep track of, and what you've to do is place yourself so that it's blowing from the badger's den right into your face. But even in such circumstances, eddies will often play you false, especially during a lull. Then the badger will take one sniff and dive into the sett like a runaway hutch down a coal mine.

He may stay below ground for an hour or more after such a scare. He may stay down for the whole night. If he does come out again he'll be more wary than ever, so if you've done nothing about the wind you'll be wasting your time.

You should decide in advance exactly how you mean to approach each sett, and once you've made up your mind you should go early —at least an hour before you expect badgers to emerge. Badgers will come out after sunset, perhaps an hour afterwards, perhaps less. In May and June the beasts will often come out in good light. Cubs will often come out in very good light.

But you can't depend on the beasts coming out early. I've had to wait until nearly midnight, in May, for Highland badgers to show. At home I have had to wait until 11.10 p.m., in June, on one night, and had them out at 10 p.m. on the next (B.S.T.). When the days are long it is always best to be in place before sunset.

If you're at a sett at 9 p.m. and no badger has emerged by 11.30 p.m., try waiting on until after midnight, for brocks can be thrawn to stir.

If you decide on a tree seat, do your building during the day, then give the badgers a couple of nights to forget about the hammering and bumping. When you're ready to have

a night out, get up to your perch an hour or more before you expect to see a badger. If you're 12 feet up you're well out of harm's way. Then sit still. Sitting still is the greatest technique of all.

A word of warning about working in a tree, if you're facing a sett which is on a slope. See that your seat is higher than the level of the den ; otherwise a wind at your back could still play you false by taking your scent straight to it. It isn't the height above the ground that matters so much ; it's the height above the badger's nose.

If your watching place is on the ground, you should gather on the spot a heap of brushwood to hide behind. The badger won't pay any attention to such familiar material. Have other brushwood screens at other points, so that you'll have a hiding-place no matter from which direction the wind is blowing. The prevailing wind on any night will determine which heap you use.

On the ground you'll have to sit motionless and make no noise. The rustling of papers, or the eating of sandwiches, are not aids to badger watching. You should behave like a piece of the scenery. On the ground, you're more restricted than when sitting up a tree.

An emerging badger usually pokes his head out, then freezes for a few moments. On dark nights his face is like a ghost rising from the earth.

In all likelihood the head will go down again after the beast has made his first test of the wind. It will reappear, and go down again. And again. Brock won't come out until he has sifted the wind carefully and assured himself that it's safe to do so.

Make no mistake about it: if the slightest whiff of your scent is carried to his nose he'll go down and stay down for an hour or more. If he comes up again, and gets the same whiff of scent, he's likely to go down and stay down for

Teaching the young idea. School-children on their first night's badger-watching.

another hour or more. At the other end of the night you can sit up and watch for badgers returning home at first light. But there should be neither sight nor smell of you to prevent the badgers coming in.

You'll see from all this that watching badgers isn't really difficult, provided you make no noise and keep yourself out of the beast's nose.

No matter how quietly you sit, you'll never persuade a badger to act contrary to the dictates of his nose.

But, having said this, let me add that badgers which have become familiar with the human scent about their den, and which have not been molested as a result, will sometimes become a bit more tolerant—to the extent of facing stray whiffs of your scent on a night of eddying puffs of wind. This

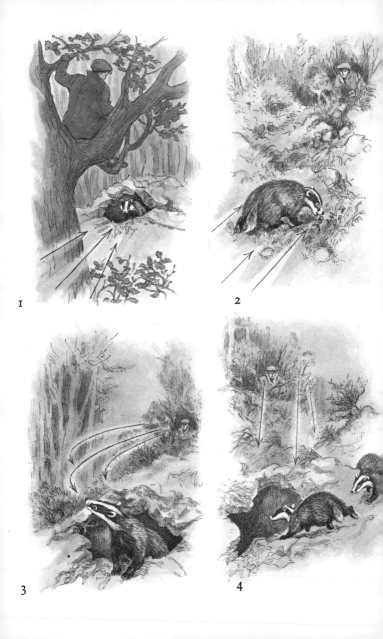

1

2

3

4

will depend on how keen they are to be out. They'll be keenest during the months of short darkness, May, June and July. Cubs will face human scent readier than their parents. But don't depend on any of them being co-operative. Take care, and proceed cautiously. When a badger gets your wind it should be an accident. Never assume he'll put up with it.

When watching badgers in the dark, you should use a red torch focused on the ground beside the hole. But don't play it right into the hole. The badger won't pay the slightest attention to the red light, and you'll be able to see him better. Once he moves clear of the den you can follow him with the light until he is out of its range. A big torch, with a deep red filter, and a diffused light, is best.

Badger cubs are far less alert than adults, and can be very naïve. Once they're at the age of playing about outside the den they can be watched quite easily so long as you don't actually frighten them.

Young cubs play a great deal, often noisily and carelessly, so that you may find them storming right up to you, and even running over your boots, without being aware of your presence. But this carefree period is short. They soon learn which scents to accept as safe and which to treat as dangerous.

You should visit a badger den during daylight, in spring, when the cubs are at the age of playing. Lie still for a while, with your ear to the ground. Cubs are often boisterously active by day, and if you listen you'll hear the bumps and rumbles of them as they roister about underground.

While it's true that badgers are mainly nocturnal, you

Opposite) *1. The watcher is well above ground, so his scent is carried gh over the badger's head.*

The watcher's presence is not suspected here because the wind is lowing from the badger to him.

The eddying wind carries the watcher's scent to the badger.

Badgers stampeding because the wind has brought the watcher's ent to them.

mustn't think for a moment that they can't be seen in daylight at any time.

Many badgers obviously like the feel of the sun. Perhaps all of them do, and it might well be that all of them would sun themselves at some time if they could do so safely. Highland badgers, especially, often have their sunning places at the den, where you can sometimes come on them dozing in the warmth.

Highland badgers, like Highland foxes, sometimes take their cubs to quiet places on the open hill far from any sett, and out there, among the heather or bracken, you may be fortunate enough to come on such a family on foot, or playing, by day. This happens more frequently than is generally realised. In some parts of the country, young badgers are

Badger cubs, three months old, emerging from the sett at sunset.

quite often run down and caught by dogs on the hill in daylight. I've found a family in the heather three or four miles from the nearest known sett or tree cover.

In any area, a well-established badger sett will be known to someone in the neighbourhood. But this doesn't alter the fact that lots of people live beside badgers for years without ever seeing one alive and free. You'll want to do better than that.

It's a good idea to list all your badger setts; then, by regular covering of the ground, note all the offshoots from them.

Near the main den, young badgers are forever digging little burrows of their own. Farther afield you'll find new burrows begun by beasts who have moved or are ready to take over new ground. In the Scottish Highlands badgers often have setts far out in the hills, and high. Try sticking all likely burrows to see if they're occupied.

Try and draw up a timetable of the movements of the badgers you're watching : when they leave the sett, and when they return in the morning, at different periods of the year. You should also note the number of nights on which no badgers emerge from a sett you know to be occupied.

The badger has an annoying habit—especially during severe weather—of gorging when he can, and then lying up for a few days and nights. He's also liable to do so in summer, staying below for a night if he's had a gorge the night before. By noting all these facts you'll soon begin to understand the ways of your particular badgers. Behaviour is by no means always the same up and down the country.

(Above) *Badger tracks in snow in mid-winter.* (Below) *Boar badger emerging from sett 1½ hours after sunset.*

How far does a badger travel in a night? Where does he hunt? These are difficult questions to answer but not unanswerable.

In winter, when there's a good tracking snow, you can follow the badger's trail, and you'll get some surprising results. You'll discover, for instance, that a mountain badger can travel a great many miles in a night, moving up and down through the contours, through the glens and over the high ridges, from 500 to 1,500 feet.

Besides betraying the badger's movements, such tracks clearly prove—if you need proof—that badgers in this country don't hibernate.

When there's no snow, or where the brock is working ground where he can't easily be tracked, finding out what he's been doing is almost impossible. Mostly, you'll know

Highland boar badger leaving sett at midnight in June.

Badger sett in mid-winter, well padded, indicating a great deal of activity at this time.

after the event. As in the case of wasps' nests, for example.

In autumn, the badger tears out a great many wasps' nests and devours the grubs. The wasps themselves don't seem to trouble him unduly, and he'll roll about in grass or corn to rid himself of them. In a good wasp year, you may find half a dozen nests which have been wrecked by a badger in a night.

If you know all the wasps' nests in advance, you can keep checking them for badger visits ; but don't expect to be at the right nest at the right time to see a badger wrecking one. I've only once come on a badger when he was busy with a wasps' nest.

A badger, as often as not, leaves his special signature wherever he's been.

If you find the quilled jacket of a hedgehog, and no other part of him, you can take it that a badger killed and ate the beast. If you find a rabbit's nest which has been raided and emptied, you can be fairly certain that a badger was the predator if it has been dug out from above. A fox digs straight in from the burrow mouth. Some badgers may do the same, but the vertical dig is a badger technique.

During periods of snow, when it's easy to find out where badgers are moving, you can sometimes see them afield or bring them to where you want them by baiting.

A few years ago I baited badgers successfully to a given place by putting down smoked fish, honey, dried horse meat, cooked flaked maize and wholewheat bread. Two of them would eat a whole basinful in a night.

I also found that, in hard weather, they would come to the pig troughs if some food was left in them overnight. I used to do this regularly, and so saw badgers almost on my doorstep. I've also persuaded badgers to use an artificial den which I built near my house.

Once, when I lived in a farmhouse, I found badger tracks

all over a snow-covered, frozen heap of sand in my stackyard. Quite obviously, what had attracted the badger was a small hole in the frozen sand. But his claws couldn't break the hard surface.

My terrier soon let me know there were rats in the hole. When I broke the crust with a pick she dug in, out of sight, and killed ten young rats and an adult. I laid all the rats aside, and hid that night at the barn window. Around midnight I had the pleasure of seeing a badger—presumably the same beast—coming back to try at the rat hole again. He ate all the rats on the spot.

Badgers will take almost any flesh food, and kill almost anything they can catch. But they're largely vegetarians, and eat such things as oats, clover, grass, bluebell bulbs, tubers, and a variety of wild fruits. They're very fond of doghips.

They like pig meal. They eat beetles and earthworms. In fact, they eat more earthworms than most people realise. Once in a while a badger will take to raiding poultry houses. Badgers are sometimes accused of killing lambs, but there is little evidence of this. A lamb at a sett isn't evidence of anything

(Opposite) *Young sow badger leaving sett at nightfall*

except that there's a fox in the den as well. Badgers don't carry food to the den.

Though he won't eat putrid flesh, as the fox does, the badger will eat any recently dead animal that takes his fancy. You can prove this by feeding a captive badger on rabbits that have been dead for several days, or venison from a deer that has been dead for a week. In other words they'll eat carrion, so long as it isn't high.

If you want to derive more from your badger-watching than the pleasure of seeing them, you should make a point of collecting scats and having them analysed to find out what the beasts have been eating.

Modern techniques have made scat analysis almost an exact science. Similarly, when you find a dead badger you should remove its stomach and have the contents analysed. If you don't know anyone who can do this for you, write to the Nature Conservancy and they'll put you on to someone.

Since badgers spend most of their lives underground, and certainly most of the daylight hours, those who die of natural causes aren't often found. Apparently they die underground, and are walled in there by the other residents. But there's

one record of a badger funeral described by Brian Vesey-Fitzgerald. In this case a dead badger was removed from the den, dragged some distance away, and buried.

I've found it worthwhile to sift through the soil thrown out by badgers during their digging. From time to time I've found the skulls and teeth of dead badgers in this way, which seems to show that underground " graves " are sometimes disturbed by future diggers. Quite recently I came into possession of two large skulls dug from the same den.

Badgers are sociable animals, and there's considerable coming and going between neighbouring setts. Presumably, these are friendly visits, deliberately contrived, but some may be due to circumstances : for example, a badger being caught far from his own home at daybreak and taking refuge in the nearest sett.

In any event, there's no evidence that a badger visiting neighbours is other than well received.

Less understandable is the behaviour of a badger who puts up with a fox as a lodger. This happens from time to time. Sometimes a hunted fox seeks refuge in a badger den. Sometimes a vixen, whose own den has been disturbed, will move her cubs there. Sometimes she'll give birth to her cubs there.

Why a badger should put up with a fox as a lodger is an open question, for the fox is a dirty housekeeper, given to cluttering up the den with remains of prey.

My own experience has been that, where there are fox cubs and badger cubs in the same sett, the foxes stick to one part and the badgers to another, and don't mix. In 1959, I watched a litter of fox cubs grow up in an occupied badger sett. They were out playing at the same time as the badger cubs but didn't play with them.

These cubs weren't molested by the adult badgers. But badgers can, and sometimes do, kill fox cubs. That's beyond question. And an adult badger can kill an adult fox when it takes the notion, as I know from personal experience. That most badgers put up with foxes is, however, true and inexplicable.

Badger cubs are born between January and April. The common months are February and March; early in the south, later in the north. Whether the adults mate in spring or autumn—and they do both—the cubs arrive the following spring. This is because of delayed implantation, already discussed in the case of the roe deer. The time of implantation may vary from badger to badger; the development time of the young is the same in them all.

THE FOX

Watching foxes presents difficulties which badger-watching doesn't. What's been said about wind, scent, noise and movement, in relation to badgers, applies equally to foxes. The main difficulty with foxes, apart from their proverbial wariness, is that you don't always know where to find them.

Unlike badgers, foxes can be found, with certainty, only at certain times of the year. Whereas the badger is an earth-dweller throughout the year, living in an established sett, the fox has far greater freedom of movement.

For a certain part of the year you can put your finger on fox cubs, more or less as you want to, because they're tied to the den for a long time, and can be seen playing about there in the months of May and June. When they're very

Six-weeks'-old fox cub photographed at daybreak.

small, the vixen lies up with them. Later, both parents carry food to them. So cub time is obviously the best time to look for adult foxes as well.

Outside this period, roughly from July until March, foxes are unpredictable.

A fox den isn't usually difficult to recognise. The most common type is an enlarged rabbit burrow. Vixens like rabbit burrows because of the easy digging. They scrape out a lot of sand, or soil, but no more than they have to, and the mound at the entrance grows much bigger than that put up by rabbits.

If you're in doubt after looking at a burrow system, there are other ways of making sure of your fox.

First, there's smell. Foxes have a strong, musky odour, and if you've a nose worth the name you should smell it the moment you poke it into an occupied burrow. The scent is so strong that you can smell it above ground under certain conditions.

It's this scent which enables hounds to follow a fox so easily, or a terrier to run one to ground on the hill.

An excited fox, or a startled fox, smells strongly. A hunted fox, it's said, gives off less and less scent as he loses strength. A fox who's neither alarmed, startled, afraid, hunted or angered, just smells like a fox.

I've often reflected, however, that a fox would be justified —if he could speak—in saying, " Men say I stink, but I can smell at half a mile a man who can't smell me at fifty yards."

Apart from fox smell, there are tracks. However much he

Working terrier with fox cub he has just killed below ground.

Highland vixen photographed by flashlight at night.

may manœuvre to kill his scent, the fox has to print his signature on every soft surface, and on the sandy soil at the den mouth this is written deeply and plainly. But you might well mistake a terrier's prints for the fox's, and there would be every excuse for your doing so.

Lots of dogs, who are neither foxhounds nor foxing terriers, poke their noses into fox holes. And they, too, leave tracks. In such circumstances it isn't always easy to pick out the prints of a fox.

But there's one way in which foxes advertise their presence, and that's the prey they leave lying about the den at cub time. Vixens aren't particular and, if prey is at all plentiful, there will be an abundance of bits and pieces lying about—birds' wings, feathers, hares' feet, beaks, claws and bones.

Where food is short, there will be fewer remains lying about. The same is true if the prey is mainly small mammals, because the cubs will devour the entire bodies. If the prey is mainly rabbits, there will be little left over, apart, maybe, from the feet.

But as soon as the foxes are on to feathered prey, or prey the size of a hare, or they're carrying home pieces of still bigger animals (for example, deer or sheep carrion) there will be plenty of remains to advertise the den.

Outside a Highland fox den I've found the fleshless leg of a red deer stag, the legs of mountain hares, the beaks of two cock capercaillies, and the remains of a curlew. Stuck in the burrow were the remains of other curlews and the feathers of a black-cock.

If it seems strange to you that such a sagacious beast as the fox should betray the whereabouts of his home by leaving prey remains lying about, the simple answer is that he does so.

As with the badger, the droppings of the fox are another guide. Foxes, however, don't dig latrines, and their scats will be found lying around all over the place.

Low country foxes—those of the lowlands of Scotland and the English shires—may den up anywhere at cubbing time: in

rabbit burrows, gravel pits, quarries or old mine workings. Yet, despite the great variety of den-sites available, there are still, in most places, sites which might be called traditional —that is to say places where you would expect to find foxes two years out of three, or even every year.

Highland foxes—tough, far-ranging outlaws with every man's hand against them for 365 days of the year—are prone to occupying traditional sites. In the hill country, the keeper knows all the likely dens. As often as not he finds his fox where he expects to find it. But foxes are always discovering new sites, or switching dens, and thus many beasts are missed each year.

In the breeding season, as you can see, it isn't too difficult to locate a vixen with cubs. But, because vixens are prone to move cubs at the slightest invasion of their privacy, the fox presents a problem you don't come up against with the badger. Badgers don't desert established setts readily. The fox will do so quickly, on the spur of the moment, if she finds human or dog scent near the den, if she's threatened or imagines she's threatened, or if she simply takes the notion.

What appears to be true is that foxes in the shires will put up with far more disturbance than any Highland tod. But, wherever your foxes live, you can't afford to be careless.

Watching cubs at a den is easy enough, especially when they're very young and, innocent. Then they may even put up with the smell of you. Since they play at the den mouth in the early evening and morning they can be watched in good light. A careful stalk is all that's usually necessary to get you within good viewing distance.

But, although young cubs will put up with a great deal, it's always best to treat them as adults from the beginning, by keeping them ignorant of your presence and not allowing them to see you for what you are.

Cubs which are undisturbed will often stay out well into

the morning and, in such cases, you can have a long spell of watching them, from daybreak until breakfast-time.

This is all very easy ; but there are complications. There always are. You can look at cubs in this careful, yet carefree, fashion, but the vixen isn't so easily fooled. While she's unlikely to put in an appearance after sunrise, she's always liable to appear with a late kill. So look out for her at all times, but especially before sunrise.

Make no mistake—her approach to the den will be determined by the wind. She'll come round until she has it full on her face, or on the side of her face. And she'll dodge about so that her nose can cover a good sweep on either side of the den. So she'll know about everything lying ahead of her, including you if you're on the ground anywhere near the den.

A vixen, startled, reacts just before her picture is taken by flash.

For this reason, if you're meaning to watch cubs early in the morning, before sunrise, you should get yourself off the ground.

If the vixen locates you—and she surely will if you're on the ground—she'll bark her warning to the cubs. And the cubs won't wait to ask what it's all about. They'll tumble below ground at once. And from the moment they learn to associate her bark with the sight or smell of you, the sight or smell of you afterwards will be sufficient to send them piling into the den without any warning bark at all.

The vixen arrives at her den at daybreak.

The older the cubs the greater care you need to take. As soon as they've learned what human beings look like and smell like they've to be treated as adult foxes.

In any case, they'll have to be treated as adults from the beginning of June, and at this time, unless you can get off the ground, you should do your watching from a distance, using field-glasses. I've been watching three months' old cubs at 4 o'clock in the morning from a distance of 120 yards, and been betrayed by the vixen coming round behind me, getting my wind, and barking her discovery.

A vixen who's still lying up with cubs can be watched in the evening or early morning if you take great care. Even if you're well off the ground, it's advisable to get back a bit, say 50 or 60 feet, because the slightest movement will alert

This badger had a vixen and her family as lodgers. The badger and fox families used separate entrances and exits.

her. The movement might make her suspicious, and if she becomes suspicious she's liable to move the family.

While a vixen isn't likely to look up, and wouldn't recognise you even if she did, so long as you were sitting perfectly still, you might make some move or sound which would betray you for what you are.

At greater distances, slight sounds and movements matter less.

It's possible—and I've done it a few times—to sit down 12 feet from a den and watch an unsuspecting vixen coming out. But there's nothing to recommend this kind of approach. It depends on your having some familiar object, such as a tree or boulder, right in front of you, and on the wind being towards you. But if the vixen takes a notion to come round behind you she'll spot you at once, and you'll never catch her like that again. Very likely she would move the family.

By and large, therefore, foxes should be watched at greater distances than badgers. Since anything you're likely to see can be seen only when the light is good enough for the human eye, there's really no disadvantage in being 20 yards away. There's every kind of disadvantage in being 20 feet away. As a matter of fact, you'd be safest at 50 yards.

With mountain foxes, viewing from a distance, using telescope or binoculars, is often forced on the watcher because of the absence of trees near at hand.

Where the den is near trees, say 200 yards or so from them, you can get aloft and watch from there. Or you can sit behind a tree, and hope that the fox won't make a wide

Fox cub, about ten weeks old, faces the camera.

enough cast to gather you in her nose when she's making her approach to the den.

Hill cubs are just as playful as any other kind, and when very young can be stalked within a reasonable distance in daylight.

Photographing a fox at a den is far more difficult than photographing a badger. Where there's plenty of cover, and a good tree handy, the difficulties aren't so great : the main one being the reaction of a vixen to a strange object such as a reflector appearing suddenly near the den.

Highland foxes are extremely difficult. Wary from persistent persecution, they'll circle all night round a den at which a strange object has appeared, trying to make up their minds about it. This is exploited by Highland fox-hunters when they want to keep a fox away from the den until the light is good enough to permit the use of a rifle. In cases where cubs have been killed the vixen is kept from making the discovery during the night then slipping quietly away. It's also exploited, where vixen and cubs have been killed, to hold the dog fox off until he can be viewed and shot in daylight.

Vixens are good mothers, and dog foxes are good fathers. A vixen will risk her life to save her cubs, and a dog fox will rear the youngsters after the vixen has been killed so long as they have been weaned 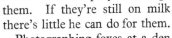 and can take the prey he brings them. If they're still on milk there's little he can do for them.

Photographing foxes at a den is a challenge. If you feel like trying it, see that you have a dummy reflector in place for some time before you use a flash. If you're working in daylight no reflector, or dummy will be necessary to obtain good results.

Although it's true that accurate analysis of fox droppings indicates what the beasts have been eating, there's every advantage in noting what you find lying about at a den. This is advisable for two reasons.

Firstly: the fox's droppings aren't all deposited near the den. Secondly: prey remains obviously aren't included in the analysis.

It isn't difficult to identify prey carried in the mouth, or prey dropped at a den after daylight or before dusk. In bad light you can use a red torch. Foxes, like badgers, don't seem to see red light. I've tried infra red, with a dull emitter, at a den near my home, but a good torch with a red filter is far better.

On some occasions, if you're near mains power, and you don't mind losing your fox if things go wrong, you could try using white light. I've tried it, but haven't pursued it as a technique, mainly because of the lighting difficulty.

The idea is simple enough. Using low-powered light to begin with (say 15 watt) you leave it on all the time at a den, or at least from before dusk until after daybreak. When the light is accepted as normal by the foxes you step up the power until you have the illumination you want.

But it's a tricky technique. You can't expect to switch on bright light at once and get away with it. Foxes aren't like that. But it's a great caper if you don't mind the risk of scaring your fox away for good.

Foxes eat an amazing variety of food, as stomach and scat analysis show. It's a great mistake to imagine that they live on poultry, game birds and rabbits. Any fox will take all of these as opportunity offers. When the rabbit was common, it was a favourite item. But the fox really has no staple diet.

Voles, mice, frogs, worms and insects, or carrion, figure large on his prey list, as they probably always have, and will. Hares are taken, both brown and mountain. Any fox will eat stoat when the alternative is stoat or hunger. Birds of many kinds are killed as opportunity offers, right up to the giant capercaillie. And poultry are killed when people are

foolish enough to allow foxes access to their henhouse. Foxes don't carry keys, and a closed house will keep them out.

He eats more worms than is generally realised. Allowed access to a food store, he'll eat cake, poultry pellets, milk powder, or fish meal. Fruit is also eaten: gooseberries, raspberries, blaeberries, blackberries, and anything else that takes his fancy.

One of the great services the fox does for the farmer is in killing rats, and it might be true to say that, in arable country and forests, he's an entirely useful animal.

I've watched a vixen carry 63 rats to her cubs in 10 nights of hunting. This den was 200 yards from my house and was fairly easy to watch. Near it was a great heap of withered potato haulms which I hollowed out and turned into a sort of igloo. This was my hiding place. The cubs ate the rats right down to the scaley tails, which they left. My count was 63 tails.

In recent years I've taken more and more to baiting for foxes. Once a beast has taken your first bait, you should keep up the supply, putting it down in daylight, with as little handling as possible and none at all if you can avoid it.

Initially, the beast will almost certainly carry the bait away.

Latterly, he may eat it on the spot, or near it, under cover, if he has no reason to be suspicious. If he keeps taking the bait away peg it down.

One of the exciting things about baiting for foxes is that you don't really know what's going to come to the bait. I've baited for a fox and found a badger. I've baited for magpies and found foxes. I've baited for badgers and found hedgehogs. And crows—in the morning. But if you keep baiting for a fox you'll usually get a fox in the end if there's one about.

Rabbits are excellent bait. So are hares. But you can ring the changes with dehydrated meat, eggs, kipper skins, and a variety of other foodstuffs. The important thing is to persuade the fox into the habit of coming and, once he's developed the habit, give him no reason to change it.

One of the advantages of baiting is that you can discover, experimentally, the capabilities of various species.

For example, if you place a bait in a tree which a fox could climb, it's quite likely that he'll climb to it. Foxes climb quite well, and sometimes hide in trees. Giving him reason to climb is probably the surest way of seeing one do so.

I've watched a fox climb 20 feet up the sloping trunk of a windblow, until he was 12 feet above the ground, to get at my roosting turkeys.

A really experienced fox will poke loose stones from a dry-stone wall to get at a prey animal hidden within—a rabbit for instance. Although many foxes are extremely reluctant to face wire netting stretched between them and a bait, or prey, others, probably familiar with it, treat it with contempt.

If you keep poultry, and are prepared to risk one or two old birds, you can learn something about foxes. Will a fox enter an empty henhouse if there's still a smell of hens in it? Try baiting him close to a henhouse. Once he's taken the bait, leave the henhouse pophole open, with a chain dangling in front of it and a couple of hens inside. Will he face the hanging chain? You can always intervene to save the birds. . . .

I recall how a neighbour's wife chased a vixen at 6 o'clock on a cold morning and recovered a hen. Mind you, the hen had no head by then. But it made good soup.

In the Highlands of Scotland, and in the hill country of the Scottish lowlands and the north of England, the fox is a problem as a predator on lambs. You cannot keep a fox away from lambs as you can keep him away from poultry. So he is a real problem animal. Most of the organised fox killing in mountain areas takes place on account of lambs.

Yet we know surprisingly little about fox predation on lambs, and this is something worth a lot of investigation. It is no use simply counting lamb carcases at a fox den; the fox could have picked them up dead. At some dens, the records show that almost all the lambs found had died of natural causes or been stillborn.

So it is necessary to know how many lambs are killed by foxes in any season, then the value of the lambs killed, then the cost of killing a fox. Otherwise we may find ourselves spending more money killing foxes than the lambs they kill are worth.

It is important to discover what foxes are eating, although this doesn't always indicate what a fox has been killing. Foxes are greater carrion feeders than most people imagine. But what they eat is important. So you should remove the stomach from any dead fox you come across. If you have sufficient interest in this animal you might collect scats as well. The Nature Conservancy will advise you how to deal with both.

January and February are the mating months for foxes, earlier in the south, later in the north.

Since the pairing season occurs at a time when there's often snow on the ground, good visibility sometimes favours the person who takes a night out on the chance of meeting a mated pair. Such encounters are rare, and mostly a matter of luck ; but if you get into the habit of sitting out on snowy, moonlit nights, in an area where fox calls are frequent, you should be favoured some time.

I've seen four foxes together on the trail of a dying roebuck, but the significance of such a gathering is obscure. But foxes do congregate where a big food carcase is available. A dead stag will attract every fox in the neighbourhood.

If you live in hunting country you should make a point of going out with the hunt—at least once. Then you'll see dog work as well as fox work. Whether you agree with hunting or not, this is part of the fox's life in certain areas, and you should see how he deals with it.

Wherever you live you should, if you're really interested in foxes, keep a terrier—a good varminty terrier who knows what he's about and is well disciplined. Such a dog, once he learns to work with you, will be invaluable when you're looking for foxes.

In the hill country, where foxes are shot, trapped, snared and poisoned, and where terriers are used for bolting vixens who are lying up with cubs, you should accompany the foxhunter when he's on his rounds looking over the dens. This is useful, because you'll see how such a terrier works, and how a big vixen behaves when the moment of truth comes for her. If you sit out with the foxhunter for a night you'll see how the dog fox behaves when he's coming in to a wrecked den. In short, whether you agree with such practices or not, it would be foolish not to see them at first hand, so long as the practices are legal.

Chance plays a big part in your approach to foxes. I once came across a fox asleep on a woodland path, and almost stepped on him before he bolted. There's a record of a

keeper who stalked into a sleeping fox and caught it by the brush.

Some years ago I learned something about the fox's relations with another predator. I was photographing eagles at the time, and one day, while spying from my hide, I saw fox cubs at a den across the glen. At intervals, when the eagles were away, I watched the fox cubs.

My watching was rewarded because, one day, the hen eagle swooped and struck, and lifted away with a fox cub in her talons. The eagle killed two cubs before the vixen moved the rest of the family.

In another year I knew another eagle who killed a whole litter of cubs and then assaulted the vixen. The vixen, however, was a wise beast, and took refuge under a boulder until the eagle tired of the ploy and flew away.

In the hill country of Scotland the paths of fox and wildcat must often cross, but a man is seldom in a position to see what happens when they do. He is, in fact, seldom in a position to see a wildcat alive and free, with or without a fox in attendance.

A brace of good terriers will find a wildcat on the hill, as they will nose out a fox, quicker than you or I could ever hope to do, and for this reason the chances of meeting either become greater if you go out regularly with your dogs, or accompany the foxhunter, stalker or shepherd to the hill.

Most wildcats which are in view for any length of time are usually run by terriers to a stop on some big crag or cliff, and that's when you can see the fireworks for which the Scottish tiger is noted. But you can add years to your age waiting for such an opportunity to come your way.

Piecing together what evidence is available—and it is scanty enough—we can reasonably assume that a fox, and more especially a pair of foxes, will hustle a wildcat as a dog will chase a tame one.

But no single fox, or even pair of foxes, can do much with a wildcat who is all set to receive such visitors. The cat is a terrible fighting machine, and a fox would have to have terribly impelling reasons to risk being cut up. One observer reported two foxes break off an encounter with a single wildcat whose fireworks and fish-hooks overawed them.

Since the ranges of fox and cat frequently overlap on the hill, there is every reason to suppose that territorial arguments crop up from time to time, and in the vicinity of the breeding dens the intruder would give way to the resident. In all other cases one would expect the cat to run from the fox in the open, in the first encounter.

THE HEDGEHOG

One of the first things you'll notice about the hedgehog if you handle one for any length of time is that he's host to a great many fleas, and it'll be surprising if some of them don't colonise you soon after you catch him up.

I mention this because, any time you find a hibernating hedgehog, you should examine him for fleas. You'll see that he can sleep his deep winter sleep while playing host to these parasites. If you've ever watched the frantic scratching of a dog, fox or badger when a flea is active, you'll appreciate how deep the hedgehog's sleep really is when so many of them leave him undisturbed. His torpor is as near death as any animal ever gets without actually dying.

Hedgehogs like eggs but have difficulty in breaking any except very small ones.

You can do one of two things with a hibernating hedgehog. You can leave him where he is—which is much the better thing to do—or you can remove him gently, and install him at home in a place of the same temperature to complete his winter sleep.

When he wakes up, which may be any time from February to March, depending on the weather, he'll be lean and drowsy, and will tend to fall asleep at any odd time until he's been a day or two on his feet.

The easiest way to study hedgehogs is to gather the number

you want, late in the autumn, let them hibernate on your premises, then give them the run of your garden in spring. Don't take hedgehogs home in spring or summer in case you remove a female who's nursing young.

If you've a walled garden, which the hedgehogs can't leave, then you'll have them under complete control while they're still living free. If they can leave the garden they may not come back. However, many hedgehogs do come back, and, once a female has given birth to her young, she'll always return.

You can't normally expect your hedgehogs to find all their food in your garden, unless it's a very big one, so you must supplement this if you want to hold them. They're not difficult to feed. Indeed, most modern dog and cat foods suit hedgehogs very well; but they will, in fact, take more or less the round of the table.

Keep careful watch on your female to see where she has her young. It'll usually be under a tree root, or in some cavity or hollow. But she'll readily choose a box or chest filled with straw if you provide it.

To begin with, the young are small and softly quilled; their quills harden as they grow.

With a family like this on your hands, you're perfectly placed to see the female suckling her young and, later on, taking them on excursions through the garden. At first she'll find the food for her young. Later, they'll find their own.

If you keep a male your female will probably breed twice, the second litter arriving in the early autumn. All these animals will hibernate with you if you give them suitable quarters. I think you'll discover that cold weather alone won't drive them into hibernation. The state of torpor comes on once the beasts have reached a certain body condition.

It has been established that the state of hibernation coincides with a reduction of the hedgehog's blood sugar. Try keeping a hedgehog at room temperature to see if this has any bearing on its time of hibernation compared with those out of doors. Try feeding it a lot of sweets—hedgehogs like chocolate—and see if this has any effect.

If you've a fish pond in your garden, or a stream running through it, you'll soon discover that your hedgehogs can swim. Sometimes they'll swim for no apparent reason. You'll also discover that they can climb rough walls, wire netting and trees; that they can fall some distance without injury because their quills act as shock-absorbers; and that they'll eat anything they can catch and hold.

Hedgehogs are only a little more difficult to watch in a wild, free state.

(Opposite) *Hedgehog defences!   At threat of danger the hedgeho curls into a tight ball with his nose tucked into his hind feet.   Phot graph shows one in process of openin*

Finding a nest isn't easy, but once you've found one it's easy to watch the comings and goings of the mother. You should note such things as the date of birth of the young, rate of growth, weight increase, and weight difference throughout the litter. Note, too, at what age the young are first able to roll themselves into a ball.

It isn't difficult to follow a wild hedgehog when he's hunting at night provided you do so carefully. You must not crowd him too close, shake the earth with your feet, cough, talk, or sneeze. You can follow him up and down a woodside, and across several fields, on foot, or on your hands and knees, without in the least alarming him. It's a matter of keeping a little way behind, and staying out of his ears and nose. The hedgehog is tolerant so long as you're not actually treading on his toes.

Following a hedgehog in this way you'll find that he catches a few frogs in ditches and boggy places. In early spring, when frogs are spawning, he'll wade or swim to catch them. Many of the hedgehogs I've watched began to eat their frog where they had a hold of it, which sometimes meant that the frog was still alive after a considerable part of it had been eaten.

You should make a point of watching any hedgehog you see in a field where dairy cows are grazing in summer. You'll find, I think, that the hedgehog will feed close to any cow that's lying down cudding. You'll also find that he likes to sniff over any place where a cow has been lying. Add this to the known fact that he's fond of milk and you have the origin of the belief that he sucks cows.

In fact, a hedgehog couldn't suck a cow if he tried, and in any case no self-respecting cow would permit it.

What the prowling hedgehog does find are the trickles of milk often pressed from an overstocked udder when a cow is lying down. The globules of milk are held for some time by the moist, pressed grass before they trickle away into the soil. Many years ago I noted, and wrote about, this. The habit has been observed by many people.

Farm stackyards are other places where hedgehogs are easily watched and followed. If a beast comes across a nest of mice or rats he'll kill and eat them all. But he'll shut himself up in his armour if he's challenged by an adult rat. In straight fight he can kill a rat weighing a pound.

The hedgehog is a considerable predator on the rabbit, killing mainly young ones still in the nest. A big male will often take over a rabbit nest after he's eaten the young : a female with young elsewhere will make return visits until she's cleaned out all the baby rabbits.

Some day you may be lucky enough to observe how a hedgehog behaves when molested by a fox. If you're not lucky enough to come on such an incident you can sometimes arrange it. In either event you'll see the hedgehog ball up at the fox's approach, and stay balled until the reynard goes away.

Foxes try all sorts of ways to make hedgehogs uncoil, most of which fail. But some foxes can manage it. One way is by rolling the hedgehog into water so that he's forced to uncoil and expose his unprotected belly.

But a persistent, knowledgeable fox can tear a hedgehog open with his teeth. He gets his grip at the chink in the hedgehog's armour where his nose and feet are tucked together. Then he pulls, and when the nose is out he bites.

You can, of course, easily observe the hedgehog's reactions to dogs and cats at any time. His role is passive defence. Nature has endowed him with an armoury of quills as a defence against his enemies and he makes use of it.

Hedgehogs eat snakes, and no doubt they kill adders; but you can't always say with certainty how a hedgehog will behave when he's brought face to face with a snake. Sometimes he attacks at once; sometimes he coils into a ball and does nothing. Try to arrange such a meeting some time and see for yourself.

Any time I've introduced a hedgehog to an adder his role has been passive, crouching with his brow quills forward while the snake struck or crawled over him. Other hedgehogs have coiled into a ball and refused to budge. An adder could make a mess of itself by striking repeatedly at a hedgehog's defences, but I haven't come across one which did this.

Hedgehogs are crepuscular and nocturnal, which means no more than that they're active mainly from dusk until daybreak. Late in the year, when the days are short, they can be seen on foot by day, feeding up before their winter sleep.

OTTERS, STOATS AND WEASELS

The otter is the sleek weasel of the water, sinuous, almost eel-like, apparently boneless as he dives, swims, twists, or rolls on the surface. When he runs on land he has the hump-backed appearance of all the weasels ; in the water or out of it he does nothing gracelessly. He is supremely adapted for his life in the water—web-footed, streamlined, with a tail that is a powerful rudder.

Shy, retiring and elusive, he is also mainly nocturnal. Though not aggressive, he is a terrible fighting machine when roused. He is also a great wanderer, travelling from river-mouth to watershed, and from one river to another, following immemorial trails, and resting where long-dead generations of otters rested on the same journeys.

The excellent Otter Report prepared for the Otter Committee by Marie Stephens contains, besides a great deal of excellent information about otters, two statements most observers would agree with : that otters are difficult to watch, and that anglers probably see more of them than most people.

It isn't difficult to understand why the angler should have been singled out for this distinction. Anglers angle where otters work. Angling is a contemplative sport. The angler stands for long periods in the water, so that he begins to appear like a piece of the landscape, a fixture on the river. With eyes, ears and mind turned to the water, he's well placed to see the elusive otter.

I'm not suggesting, however, that in order to see otters you should take up angling.

It may be that you'll take up angling, if you haven't already done so. As a result you can expect to see more of the otter than most people. But you can see more otters than most people without taking up angling.

I'm not an angler, but if I want to look for otters every day, for weeks on end, I can do so, simply by making up my mind, and without having to introduce the complication of trying to catch fish.

What you require is the angler's temperament : his ability to stay still, doing nothing, with body relaxed and eyes and ears on the alert. This won't automatically produce more otters, or bring otters to where you are. But when one does come along you'll be well placed to see as much of him as he's likely to see of you.

All this changes once you've found a holt that's occupied. What you've to become then is the cautious and painstaking observer, and it doesn't matter whether you know how to catch fish or not.

An otter holt is a lying-in place, a den, or a nursery,

depending on the time of year and the movement of otters on the river. At any time the holt will be used for one or other of these purposes—not by one otter all the time, but by different individuals as they travel up and down the river, and by succeeding generations following traditional trails.

Once you know a holt, and that there are otters in the neighbourhood, you know that you'll have one beast in a predictable place at some time.

Otter cubs may be born in any month of the year, but recent investigations have shown that most of them are born in the spring. When the cubs are very small, you'll see little of the bitch otter beyond her coming and going. You'll have long waits, and might well wish you were somewhere else angling.

The best place to be when you're watching a holt is in the branches of a riverside tree. It's important to get off the ground, or in some place where otters aren't likely to smell you or bump into you.

Your seat should be prepared against the time when the cubs will be big enough to take to the water. Then you'll have a chance of seeing the bitch with them—swimming, diving, hunting and coming ashore.

It is a fact that otter cubs don't take willingly to the water. They have to be cajoled, or pushed in. But the parents don't teach them to swim. They need no such teaching, any more than a duckling does. They don't make a glad rush for the water, but they know

187

what to do once they're in it. Otters hunt mainly at night, except when food is scarce. In a hungry season you might see one in good light, on shore, perhaps far from the water.

When there's snow on the ground, the otter leaves a plain trail with a distinctive signature. You should follow such tracks whenever you can. Sometimes, they lead over many miles of country, far from river or stream. In the Scottish Highlands you'll find tracks going right over the tops from one glen to another, in mid-winter.

Tracks may lead to rabbit warrens, or into farm stackyards, for the otter takes rabbits, mice, rats and anything else he can find. He'll take poultry, ducks, or turkeys when faced with famine.

Some years ago, during a savage spell of frost and snow, I watched (from a hide) an otter killing a mallard duck on a frozen lochan in bright moonlight. Every movement of the beast was perfectly visible—the stalk, the kill, and the otter's subsequent dispossession by two foxes. That was the arctic winter of 1947. I had not seen the like before, and I don't expect ever to see the same again.

Otter hunters, who follow hounds on foot, see a good deal of their quarry ; but hunting isn't watching, although it does teach the hunter much about the hunted animal.

On the other hand, the man who traps otters learns little about them, because the beasts are broken in his traps, or dead, when he finds them.

The angler, perhaps, comes off best because, when he sees an otter, it's usually doing something without being compelled to do so—playing, fishing, or even rising to try for the fish on the angler's line.

You don't have to see otters fishing to know what they're eating, although, of course, it's more fun seeing them. Their droppings, called spraints, can be analysed to give a reliable

index of food eaten. So you
should collect spraints, and
the stomachs from any dead
otters you find.

Otters found near the sea in
this country aren't sea otters.
The sea otter is a different
species altogether.

The otters of the Western
Isles of Scotland spend much of
their time in the sea, and they
eat a lot of marine life, in-
cluding shellfish; but they are the ordinary otters you
meet elsewhere in Britain. When they are not in the sea
they make journeys up and down the short rivers. Their
travels are limited by geography, but the impulse is still
there.

Whatever else they may eat, the food of otters is mainly
fish. They prey to a very great extent on eels. They take
salmon, and trout, of course; but otters make no significant
difference to the stock of a salmon river. If salmon become
scarce it won't be because of otters. A fish pond is different.
There an otter can wreak havoc. Then he is the fox in the
henhouse all over again, and has to be summarily dealt
with.

If you come across an otter slide you should try to keep an
eye on it. Otters are playful. Such slides are usually on
steep banks—slippery slopes of flattened grass in summer
and snow slides in winter—and there the otters glissade and
play. You may watch for a long time without seeing any
otters. But you could be lucky. It's worth some lost sleep
to take a chance.

Your approach to an otter slide should be made in daylight.
And you shouldn't go too near it. If you decide to watch

for a spell, get off the ground where you can have a good view, and be prepared to stay the night.

Otters, like foxes and other mammals, have an irritating habit of not doing what you expect while you're watching, then doing it the moment your back is turned. At least that's how it always seems. The point is that you'll have to spend much time and expend much effort for little return. But that's the way of it with otters. If the fox is less accommodating than the badger, the otter is less so than the fox.

When I lived in my farmhouse, there was a pond nearby much frequented by moorhens. These birds are often the prey of the otter. One of the otter's methods of catching a moorhen is to dive and come up under it, then pull it under the surface. For many nights I watched this pond from dusk till dawn, hoping to see this. I saw moorhens, but no otters.

When I finally did see it happen, I wasn't watching the pond at all. I was passing by with my dogs, when I saw a moorhen being pulled under the surface of the water. A few seconds later the otter came ashore with the bird in her jaws. So you see the luck of being in the right place at the right time often gives better returns than fifty hours of trying. Yet, in the long run, trying is the only sure way of seeing most things.

Bear in mind that otters can have cubs at unlikely times of

the year. I've seen a bitch with half-grown cubs in March, when the frogs were spawning ; in fact, she was catching frogs at the time. And I've seen small cubs late in September. So you can never be sure.

Nor can you ever have much certainty with the stoat and the weasel. These two small members of the Mustelidae (relatives of the rare pine marten and polecat) are difficult to put your finger on—not so difficult once you've caught up with them.

Both are very curious, even concerning man. This curiosity is often the death of them ; but it has many advantages for the man who wants to study them.

Any time you see a stoat or weasel running into a hole in a wall you shouldn't pass on thinking you've lost it. Stand by and wait for it to reappear ; as often as not that's what it will do. The weasel that has taken refuge in an old dry-stone wall can hardly get out quickly enough to look at the person he ran away from in the first place.

If the person waiting by happens to be a man with a gun, and the wrong idea, the weasel is dead. If the person is interested in weasels for their own sake, he'll have view after view of this elusive, quick-moving little animal before it tires and disappears.

If you come across either stoat or weasel carrying a prey, you should move quickly towards it. Very often it will drop the prey and dart into cover. If this happens, you should withdraw a little way and wait for the animal to return.

In most cases the beast will return for its prey. You can test its persistence by making it drop the prey several times, and watching it return again and again. The hungrier it is the more persistent it will be. But you must judge the moment when to leave it in peace ; otherwise, if you overdo things, it will leave without it.

If you find a newly killed weasel on a road—or if a car in

which you're travelling kills one—it's a good plan to stand by for a while and watch. If the weasel you found newly killed, or have just killed, was one of a family party, it's more than likely that the others will come back and drag the body under cover. If the dead beast was alone when killed there's no point in waiting.

Stoats behave similarly in such circumstances, so you have to be able to tell the one from the other.

The stoat is a much bigger animal than the weasel, and has a bushy tail tipped with black at all times. The weasel has a short, smooth tail with no black tip. In winter, any white "weasel" will be a stoat. In the British Isles the weasel doesn't change to white. It does so in more northern latitudes.

A word of warning about these quicksilver, explosive little mammals. It's inadvisable to push your bare

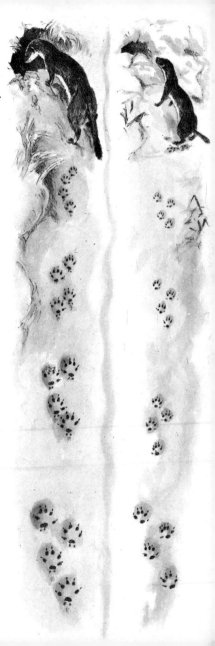

(opposite) *Male stoat in typical hunting attitude.*

hand into a burrow where you know a stoat or weasel to be, or where you think one may be, because there's every chance that you'll be promptly bitten. For the same reason you should be careful about pressing too close on a family party or other group. They might resent it. This is certainly true of the stoat, in winters when small packs are roaming the countryside. I've been bitten. So have other people.

This is no more than a warning not to take too much for granted. It doesn't mean that you should go about in fear of stoats. Most mammals will fight back when cornered or threatened, or when they think they're cornered or threatened.

Both stoat and weasel come readily to a bait. There's no need to use a live bait. Apart from being cruel it isn't necessary. A freshly dead bird, a mouse, a rabbit, a chick, an egg, or a piece of raw meat will do.

Stoats and weasels take a variety of food: rats, mice, voles, small birds, the chicks of bigger species, eggs, rabbits and leverets. Either will enter a building that is swarming with rats ; both are rat-killers of the first order. A 4-ounce weasel will kill a rat weighing a pound and a quarter. It can kill three in fifteen minutes, as I have seen.

The stoat will store food. Where one is gathering eggs into a cache you have a ready-made place for watching. The stoat will pay little attention to you if you remain still.

If you know of a nest of stoats or weasels in your neighbourhood, it's a simple matter to bait the adults any time you want to. If they're near your home it's easier still. Weasels will come

(Above) *Female weasel squeaks defiance from a wall top.* (Below)
*Weasel hunting in drainpipe. Drains and tunnels of all kinds
attract this hunter.*

to your bait by night or day; stoats come mostly at night. Place the bait in some kind of tunnel, or archway—you can make one of stones or use a drainpipe—for both animals like such alleyways.

Once you've found a nest of stoat or weasel the adults will come and go readily, even when you're close by, so long as you don't frighten them unduly or give them too much of your scent.

If you keep careful watch on such a nest you'll be able to tell, pretty nearly, the day when the young ones will be ready to leave and go hunting with their mother. Such a family makes up the summer pack. Probably the winter pack too.

Stoat with rabbit. When rabbits were plentiful they were a favourite prey item of this species.

The stoat in winter dress becomes the ermine.

Stoats breed once a year, weasels probably twice. In the stoat we meet again the phenomenon of delayed implantation, already noted in the roe deer and the badger.

Stoats and weasels are territorial animals, and you will find both occupying the same ground at the same time. The males are the territory holders, and they defend their ground against other males of their own kind. But not against other species. The females settle and live within the males' territory, but hunt only part of it. Once they have a family, they hunt all of it. Stoat and weasel kits, once they are self-supporting, are driven from the parental territory and become wanderers in search of a place to settle.

Any time you hear the scream of a rabbit in the night, you

should hurry to investigate. The animal may have been caught by a stoat, and a stoat can drag a rabbit quickly under cover. If the rabbit has been killed by a stoat, and the stoat runs off at your approach, stand by and wait for it to return. Then you can watch the carry-away or the drag, depending on the size of the rabbit.

If you come on a stoated rabbit at any time—an otherwise healthy rabbit that crouches and allows you to stroke and handle it without a struggle—you should wait on in case a stoat arrives to take the prey.

Stoats are often to be seen about rabbit warrens, and this is where you're most likely to see one hunting a selected animal and ignoring others nearby.

Stoats that live in rabbit warrens sometimes play with their neighbours. I've seen this once. When you're having a spell of watching at a warren you may see it too.

BIRDS BY NIGHT

WHEN PEOPLE speak of the wise old owl they are referring entirely to appearances. Owls, indeed, look wise. In fact, they're not very bright, even by bird standards—certainly not to be compared with the crow family for intelligence.

Without for a moment suggesting that you should treat owls as simpletons, I would say that you'll find them among the easiest of birds to observe at close quarters. The difficulty with owls isn't the birds ; it's the conditions under which you've to work.

How is one to do much with a bird that flies mainly after dark ; that can see in the dark much better than you or I ; that has extraordinarily acute hearing ; and that flies without making the slightest sound ?

You might think that all these things would make owl-watching extremely difficult, and unprofitable as a pastime. In actual fact, you'll discover that the difficulties aren't nearly as great as they seem.

Let's look first at the tawny, or brown, owl—a common

Tawny owl arriving at nest with prey—flashlight.

species and the one Shakespeare was referring to when he wrote :

> *Then nightly sings the staring owl,*
> *Tu-whit, tu-who, a merry note. . . .*

Although this species is usually described as a woodland nester—as indeed it is—it would be a great mistake to imagine it nests nowhere else.

You'll find the tawny nesting in isolated trees, in rabbit burrows in or out of woodland, sometimes even in old buildings. In the Scottish Highlands you'll sometimes find it nesting in rock holes at ground level, far out on the open hill. But, by and large, woodland is certainly the place to look for the tawny owl.

If there are hollow trees available it's more than likely that you'll find your owl in one of these. If there are none, or the birds are obviously not using any hollow tree in the neighbourhood, you must look for them in the old nests of other birds : crow, magpie or sparrowhawk.

It isn't difficult to establish whether or not there are owls in any strip of woodland. Obviously, if you visit the place at night, you'll hear them calling sooner or later. The tawny is the species with the eerie, bubbling hoot, and the clear, incisive *Kee-wick, kee-wick*, which sounds like an Indian war whoop.

By day, you can seek the birds at roost. Tawny owls usually sit close to the main stem of the tree, drawn up tall. Cold searching will eventually lead you to your owl, but the

Tawny owl asleep on her nest by day.

Pylon hide erected for photographing tawny owl.

presence of pellets on the ground under trees will narrow your search.

Owl pellets are composed of the indigestible matter—fur, bones, teeth, feathers and the like—put up by the birds, and you may find from 2 or 3 up to 50 or more scattered about under one tree. In woodland, the presence of pellets will not at once tell you what species of owl you're dealing with. You'll have to look, but it will almost certainly be either a long-eared or a tawny as these are the woodland species.

From the moment you begin to take an interest in owls you should make a habit of collecting pellets, noting the place and the time of year. Then you should have the pellets analysed.

You can do this in a rough way yourself, and get fairly accurate results. For example, the presence of a small skull with teeth indicates a small mammal, probably a vole or a shrew. If you take the pellet apart you'll discover other bones. A bird's beak is easily recognised. Fur and feathers remain quite obviously fur and feathers.

But if you want to know exactly the prey species represented in owl pellets you should have them examined by an expert.

Besides playing the detective for you, he will quickly point out to you how to identify certain items for yourself.

Where there are owls there have to be pellets. Some trees will have lots of pellets round about them. Though tawny owls may change their day-roost from time to time, it will often be betrayed by the presence of pellets.

Another way of finding your owl is to listen to the calls of other birds. If you hear the alarm call of a blackbird, for instance, or the sudden scolding of a magpie, especially late in the day, the birds may have spotted an owl. If they're interested in a certain tree that's where your owl is likely to be.

Very often, when an owl rouses itself at dusk to begin hunting, a blackbird will announce the fact to the world in unmistakable, staccato alarm notes. And you can take the blackbird's word for it. . . .

The tawny owl nests early, usually some time in March. The eggs are laid at intervals of two days, sometimes longer. Since the bird begins to brood as soon as she has laid her first egg, the owlets hatch out at two-day intervals, or according to the time-lag between eggs.

The usual number of eggs is three. But some owls will lay four and hatch four. Occasionally a bird will lay five eggs, hatch five, and rear five owlets to the flying stage. Abundant food is essential for nesting success of this order, and a nest with five owlets is a busy place, well worth watching at night.

You should be looking for your owls by the beginning of April. A tap with a stick on the trunk of a likely tree will send the bird out of the hole or off the nest as the case may be. Once you have discovered her in this way, or in any other way, you should leave her in peace until after hatching time.

Generally speaking, the harder an owl is sitting the less

Tawny owlets waiting to be fed at nest in hollow tree.

readily she will go off, so, if an owl doesn't fly out at once, don't go hammering on the tree as though you were trying to fell it. You can visit that tree much later, and climb it, if you haven't found the nest elsewhere in the interval.

If you visit the owls by day, and put up the cock from his roost, you should watch where he flies and follow him. When you put him up again he will continue to fly away from you. But, presently, he will reach a point where he will turn about and fly past you in the reverse direction. You should try this, because it has been established that this turning point indicates the boundary of the bird's territory on that side.

In some cases, the bird will reach this boundary very quickly ; in others he will fly some distance, because the territory is a large one. Where owls are on the ground in numbers territories may be very small. In open country,

with scattered plantings, territories will be big and the boundaries very elastic.

On an evening when the light is good you should try watching a hunting owl to see how much ground he covers. Recently, I was watching a pair who hunted over a square mile of hill, up to 1,000 feet. So you should try pushing the owl out as far as he will go, repeating the process on other days and in other directions, to get some idea of the size of his territory.

It is often possible to watch the owls in fairly good light, because they aren't strictly nocturnal. They will fly before dusk, and sometimes in the middle of the day in the subdued light of a wood, especially when they have hungry owlets in the nest and the previous night's hunting was poor.

Late-nesting tawny owls are even more prone to hunt in good light because the nights are so much shorter in summer. Great pressure is put on birds with owlets hatched late in May, and I have seen tawnies carry prey to a nest at 2 p.m. in that month.

What applies to evening light applies also to early morning. The owls will hunt well on towards sunrise if they have to. So, if you are seated in a convenient place just before sunrise, or towards sunset, you may see something of the birds' movements.

You may find, by watching the cock regularly at this time (he is the one who is always free because he doesn't sit on the eggs), that he has a place to which he flies regularly, for example, a farm stackyard. If a stackyard is one of his hunting stations you can be sure of seeing him at work if you hide there.

He may not come to the stackyard in good light, preferring to wait until after dark. But this needn't prevent you from

Long-eared owl brooding owlets by day.

seeing him because, sooner or later, he will pitch on top of a stack or tree, silhouetted against the sky. In any case, your eyes will have become accustomed to the poor light and you'll be surprised at how well you can see. As an aid, you can use a red torch if you like. This won't upset the bird at all and will help you to see better what he is doing.

Stackyards are also good places at daybreak, and I've had some interesting encounters with owls at that time of the morning.

But, of course, the real business of getting to grips with owls has to be done at night. The nesting season is the best time, and near the nest is the best place.

The simplest way to learn something about owl behaviour at this time, and the one involving least trouble, is to choose a seat on the ground which gives you a good view of the nesting site, and isn't too far away. Twenty yards is a good distance.

At the chosen place you should put up a screen of branches or brushwood, preferably against a tree trunk. If you get tired of sitting and want to stand, the tree trunk will hide you. Behind this cover, sitting or standing, you won't upset the owls so long as you don't move. Either they won't see you, or they'll pay no attention to you.

You should be in your position before sunset if you want to try this; if you're a fidget you shouldn't go closer than fifty yards.

If there are hungry owlets in the nest, and the night is fine but not too bright, the cock will begin hunting at the earliest possible moment.

At first, you may not be able to tell just when he begins

Cock long-eared owl arrives at nest with prey at 2 a.m.

hunting ; but you'll soon learn to tell the moment of his arrival with the first prey of the evening. When he arrives in the wood he will probably hoot, and soon you will hear him in the vicinity of the nest. In all probability he'll pitch in some tree near to it, and you'll hear his *kee-wick* call from there.

Once you've discovered what tree he pitches in, you can watch it afterwards, for he'll usually come to it with food and call to the sitting hen from there.

If the owlets are very small, or haven't all hatched, or the night is cold, the hen owl may refuse to leave the nest. If she ignores his calling, and stays, the cock will fly to the nest with the prey in his beak. And this is when you're likely to hear a kind of conversation-piece of cat-calls between them.

At other times, the hen will fly from the nest when summoned and take the prey from the cock. In either case, the cock soon leaves to resume his hunting.

Once in a while the hen will fly out with the cock after he has delivered the prey, and they will circle about for a few minutes, calling loudly. Then she will return to the nest and feed the owlets on the prey.

You should try to discover when the first owlet is due to hatch, or is hatching. That same daylight have a look in any old nest in, or near, the cock's roosting tree. You may find nothing unusual. On the other hand you may find some item of prey. I know no more than this : some cock owls do hold prey close at hand at this time.

When I first came across this, I thought it was simply exceptional behaviour. I found the old nest of a crow which contained the haunch of a small rabbit and a fresh shrew. Both appeared in the owl's nest the same night, when the first owlet was only a few hours out.

Twice, in other years, I came across the same thing. No

more. The habit may be exceptional. But tame owls do store food, and remember where they store it. And why shouldn't an owl lay aside surplus prey? I can't be more definite than this, but it's something you might well look out for as you go along.

The long-eared owl is a woodland species, more strictly nocturnal than the tawny. But it can be watched in exactly the same way.

In this case, however, most of your observations will be carried out in bad light, or in total darkness. But you can, of course, use a red torch and train it on the tree.

Another drawback is that long-eared owls are far less vocal than tawnies. But you'll soon learn to recognise their distinctive hoot, which is low-pitched and soft, almost breathless, even at times like a sigh.

The long-eared likes dark woods, especially coniferous woods. The technique of finding the nest is the same. This species usually chooses the old nest of crow, magpie or sparrowhawk. But you'll also find it nesting on the ground, under a tree root, in a hole at the base of a tree, or among tall grass or reeds. Most nests are, however, in trees.

The short-eared owl presents its own particular difficulties because it haunts open ground—moorlands, hillsides and reed flats—and nests on the ground.

It hunts habitually by day, which is a help. But it also sees well by day, which means it's an alert bird by day. You might say it has, therefore, no " dozey " time. Generally speaking, if you want to get to grips with this species you've to watch from a distance, or build yourself a hiding place on the territory, using whatever growth is available as camouflage.

The barn owl, mainly because of its close association with human dwellings, is perhaps the easiest of all to work with. Although you'll find it nesting in hollow trees (the kind of place where you'd expect to find the tawny), most barn owls nest about farm buildings or ruins. Church towers and old dove-cotes also attract them. And, since they hunt the farmyard and surrounding fields, very often when the light is good, and sometimes by day, they are easily watched in the early evening and early morning.

Everything that has been said so far has been directed towards getting you to grips with owls in a general way. What you'll want to do after that is something you'll decide for

yourself. But if the owl magic catches you, it's almost certain that you'll want to make a closer acquaintance. This requires organisation, and much more care.

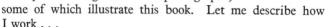

When I became seriously interested in owls 25 years ago, I built all sorts of high hiding places so that I could sit up beside them. Originally I built merely to observe ; latterly I built again to take photographs, some of which illustrate this book. Let me describe how I work . . .

Suppose I have been keeping watch on the nest of a tawny owl on the ground. I know where the cock roosts, where he puts up pellets, and where he pitches when he comes in with prey at night. But I want to get closer : to observe the birds at the nest, to check what prey is being brought, and to watch the hen feeding her owlets. I set about building a hiding-place.

This hiding-place, which will eventually be erected about 12 feet from the nest, has to do two things. It has to conceal me and it must never upset the birds. This means gradually changing the landscape with which the birds are familiar, and I do this in one of two ways, depending on the lie of the ground.

The best way, and the safest way, is to build a hide 25 yards or so from the nest, and move it in gradually at one move per day—say five yards at a time—until it's in the required position.

If I have to erect a hide on the spot where it's wanted, I put it up a little bit at a time : a small heap of local material the first day, which becomes a bigger heap on the second, and bigger still on the third. By the time this is 3 feet or so high I replace it with my hide, draping the local material over it, and fixing it firmly in place.

I finish up with a hide about 5 feet high and 3½ square. It's important to build gradually, and I do so in daylight because that's the time the owls pay least attention to scene-changing.

For my hides I use strong posts, firmly planted in the ground, as uprights, and hessian as covering. This is camouflaged with the local material—bracken, branches, or grass as the case may be—which is pinned down securely. The hide has to be free from flap, so it's often necessary to weight the bottom down with stones.

On level ground the hide will be squared, even and trim. When the owls have their nest on a slope this can't be done, and improvisation becomes necessary. But the rules are the same.

There's no reason in the world why a hide like this should upset the owls, and absolutely no excuse if it does.

When I am ready to work I go into my hide before sunset, making as little disturbance as possible. Invariably I have someone with me who will leave after I have been installed, advertising his departure as much as possible. Owls aren't fools, but they are easily fooled by this arrangement. Although they may observe two persons arriving at the nest they can't tell that only one has left.

The golden rule is that a hide should be accepted as part of the normal scene. If the watcher enters a hide unaccompanied the owls will become suspicious if they see no one leaving. And the last thing he wants is to have the birds connect the hide with human beings.

If the owlets are small, I expect the hen owl back on the nest within minutes of my companion's departure. If the chicks are partly grown I expect her to take a little longer. But I know she will be back. When she does fly on, she settles down at once, and all I have to do is wait for something to happen.

When I hear the cock hooting nearby—a wonderful and startling call—I know he has arrived with prey. The loud, liquid and brief hoot with which the cock announces his arrival near the nest is quite different from the faint, quavering cries he utters when he is flying his rounds. When he gives his *kee-wick* call, to which the hen may, or may not, reply, I expect him in at any moment, unless the hen flies off to him.

By now I know where the cock pitches, so sometimes I can look at him through a peephole in my hide, after illuminating the spot with a red light. In this way I have watched him flying in to the nest with prey in his beak.

The prey is often a mouse, or vole, or shrew. But it may well be anything of similar size : a baby rabbit, a young rat, a small weasel, a peewit chick or curlew chick. Or an earthworm.

The hen owl doesn't stand aside to feed her chicks. With the prey underneath her, she feeds them without uncovering them. The watcher can hear the owlets chirping, and see momentary flashes of white down, but that is all. Once the owlets have been fed, the hen will either swallow the remains of the prey herself or keep it beside her for future use.

If you have a hide say 12 or 15 feet from an owl's nest on the ground, you'll be able to tell how many prey items are brought to it in a night. You'll be able to record when the owlets begin to feed themselves. And you'll see them swallowing small mammals whole, with much gulping and grimacing.

In the early part of an evening you'll see all you need to see with your unaided eyes, but as the night grows dark you may want a light. This light should be dull red, and firmly fixed to one of the uprights, so that the mere pressure of a switch plays the beam on and round the nest, without any noisy manœuvring.

I've pointed out that tawny owlets, generally speaking, hatch at two-day intervals, so you might note how the smallest chick makes out when food is plentiful and when it is scarce.

If the youngest owlet dies, note the conditions prevailing at the time—scarcity of food, weather and so on. Is there any connection between wet nights and bad hunting ? What age was the youngest owlet at death ? Was its body used as food for the others ?

After 24 hours or longer of almost constant rain, it's a good plan to spend part of the following day with the owls to see if they're active—hunting, or carrying prey to the nest, in daylight.

If you feel like it you could colour-spot each owlet on the white down of its crown : one red, one green, one yellow and so on. Then you'll know which bird is which. And this is a useful thing to know.

All this is easy enough where your owl has her nest on the ground. When she is high up in the old nest of a crow, or in a hole in a tree, 10 or 12 feet from the ground, the difficulties begin.

When I want to get close to a bird in a hole 10 or 12 feet from the ground, I erect a pylon 8 feet high and put my hide on top. I use good, sound timber for uprights, 2 x 2 or 3 x 2 inches, and good floor boards. Cross members from top to bottom make the whole structure secure. I see that the hide can be opened and closed easily, because there will be times when I'll want to enter it or leave it in the dark.

If you feel inclined to work at such a nest, see that you

build piecemeal so as not to alarm the owls. And see that your structure is strong.

The wooden uprights can be completed at one visit, during the day, because the owl won't heed them. The building of the actual hide has to be done slowly, over several days, and in daylight. But, although you have to build slowly, in the sense of adding only a little each day, you have to work quickly while you are there.

Be ruthless with yourself about the length of time you spend at the nest. If the owlets are small, work in the middle of the day, and limit yourself to twenty minutes on any one day. Don't work while the owl is on eggs ; wait until she has chicks out. And always leave a margin of safety, no matter what you're doing. Owls will tolerate a lot, but that is no excuse for pushing them.

Where the owl is high up in a tree, you would be well advised to forget about it unless you know exactly what you are doing. Far better, at the beginning, to get some kind of guidance from an older and more experienced head. But if you must get up aloft there are two ways of doing so.

If there's a nearby tree with strong, spreading branches, it's often possible to rig up a hide of sorts on these, and make it comfortable. More often than not the nearby trees don't give you a good view of the nest. The answer then is a high pylon, and building this requires much labour from several hands and a lot of timber.

To begin with, you would be well advised to forget about high nests and concentrate on those on the ground, or low down in hollow trees. Sitting high has many advantages in other directions as I'll explain, but none for watching owls.

Watching long-eared owls is the same as watching tawnies, but the long-eared is more strictly nocturnal, and most nests will be in tall trees. Some birds do, however, nest on the ground and this is the kind of nest you should look for.

If you have to get into a tree be careful how you work and make sure not to disturb the birds unduly. Build carefully, because you will be risking your neck.

Unlike the long-eared and the tawny, the barn owl often makes things easy for the watcher by nesting indoors : in barn, tower, ruin, loft or dovecote. With a roof over your head it's easy to make yourself comfortable for a night's vigil. And barn owls in buildings have a high tolerance of human beings.

For the barn owl, you should make your hide by rearranging the scenery in the loft or barn. And you can do this pretty well at one move. But if you've to provide all the material, or most of it, from elsewhere, it's best to make the change more gradually.

Once the owlets have hatched you can move in. A good plan is to fit a low-powered red light into the nearest socket, or run a wire to a point near the nest and fit a small bulb there. You can leave this on all night for a couple of nights before you begin watching ; then you can see your owls in good lighting which doesn't upset them.

The birds can be built up to accepting ordinary illumination, but this is too distracting. It is also unnecessary.

With the barn owl you'll never be short of pellets to analyse because they'll be lying all around the " nest ", often several inches deep.

The little owl, an alien species, is well established in many parts of England. In recent years it has gained a foothold in the south of Scotland. It's no more difficult to watch than the native owls.

Fortunately, it frequently nests very low, a favourite place

(Opposite) *Little owl with owlet at entrance to nesting hollow in riverside tree. The little owl is an alien which has spread over most of England and is now in process of colonising Scotland*

being holes in pollarded willows. It also nests in rabbit burrows, holes in walls, under roof tiles, in sandpits, and sometimes in the old nests of other birds.

This small owl is extremely vocal, and an orchestra in itself. If you want to hear cat calls, yelps, hisses, barks, whistles and demonic laughter you should spend a night or two out of doors on the territory of a pair of nesting little owls. If you're seated half a dozen yards or so from the nesting hole, under cover, you'll have the birds performing in your ear.

During the nesting season the bird sometimes hunts by day. Habitually, it hunts in the early evening, and well on into morning light. So if you're hidden near the nest you'll often have a clear view of the bird without the aid of red lighting.

Putting up a hiding place presents no problems. The work should be done in daylight, when the bird is in the nest with her owlets. Treat her as you would a tawny owl nesting on the ground.

The little owl feeds on earthworms, beetles, moths, spiders, small mammals and birds. Individual owls take the chicks of partridge and pheasant, and so aren't liked by those who preserve game. But it is doubtful if predation by this species makes any difference at all to the numbers of game birds on their territory.

By day, you'll often see the little owl, a squat dwarf, perched on roadside poles, walls or hedges. In flight, despite its buoyant, bouncing action, it is obviously an owl. On the ground it can run as fast as a mole, as you'll see if you watch one snapping up worms on a lawn.

Individual little owls, despite their small stature, can handle big prey. I've never been lucky enough to see any feats of strength myself. I've seen thrush and blackbird in a nest-hole, but only insects, earthworms and spiders carried there. Yet prey the size of the woodpigeon has been recorded —a staggering tackle for such a small predator.

The short-eared owl, which nests in open country, can be observed by day. Getting close to this species is best done by building a hide some distance away and moving it in by stages.

You'll find that young short-eared owls begin to crawl about in the heather or grass long before they're able to fly. But they won't usually go far, and you'll still be able to watch the old birds feeding them.

The old owls will plot for you the position of the wandering owlets at any time. Where an adult drops with prey you'll find an owlet. Not infrequently a short-eared owl will perform a distraction display, and thus betray the presence of owlets. Some birds will display from eggs. Keep track of the owlets, noting if any of them falls a prey to ground predators such as fox or stoat.

In years when voles are numerous, short-eared owls often nest in colonies. When there are large numbers of owlets moving about on the ground, foxes are often tempted to prey on them, and do prey on them. Seated on the ground you won't be likely to see many foxes ; but you could be lucky. In any case, note how many owlets disappear from the local population.

Recognising owls away from the nest, or in flight, is a knack you'll acquire as you go along.

Size betrays the little owl : it is only 8 inches long.

The short-eared owl is long-winged, with a wide spread. It flies by day over open country.

The barn owl is the ghost owl, always betrayed by the amount of white, which shows in any lighting.

The tawny owl appears front-heavy in flight, due to its big head.

The long-eared is slimmer and paler than the tawny. Its

ear tufts don't show in flight. Once it pitches it erects them. So if you are seeing an owl in silhouette, and it suddenly sprouts horns, it will be a long-eared.

Any time you come across an unattended owlet on the ground don't assume that it has been abandoned, or that it's "lost." Most owlets become lost only when somebody "rescues" them, then abandons them. Generally speaking, an owlet on the ground is best left where it is, if it's well grown. If it's very tiny, obviously too young to keep itself warm, you can look for the nest and put it back.

Young short-eared owls should never be lifted ; the ground is their home.

Very small tawny or long-eared owlets, which have fallen, or have been pushed, from the nest, are usually ignored and soon die. Bigger owlets, able to call to the parents, are usually looked after by them on the ground. So don't take away any owlet unless you're certain it has been dropped there by someone. A big tawny owl will soon let you know whether the owlet you're looking at is lost or not. She'll whoop at you and perhaps swoop at you.

The tawny owlet has dark, shining eyes. The barn owlet has dark eyes, too, but its plumage is white and buff. The short-eared owlet has yellow eyes with a black pupil, and the long-eared, orange eyes with a black pupil. Small size betrays the little owlet, which has yellow eyes with a black pupil.

And now a word of warning. When studying owls at night, you'll be taking a risk with only one species : the tawny. This owl doesn't hesitate to swoop and strike at human intruders, especially after dusk but often by day. Therefore, when you are near the nest of a tawny owl at night, you should make a habit of wearing some kind of eye shields. This is absolutely imperative because, if the owl flies at your face, you will neither see nor hear her. I've been taloned in the ear and face by a tawny, and Eric Hosking, the famous bird photographer, lost an eye. As an added precaution I hold a lighted torch in my teeth when climbing up or down an owl's tree after dusk but this doesn't always keep the bird off.

Sooner or later, in the course of your owling, you're going to come on an owlet which has been injured or maltreated by someone, or taken from its home area by someone then abandoned, and very likely you'll have to take care of the bird yourself.

If you do this, the owl is going to grow up tame, which means it will go about its normal affairs undisturbed by your prying or your presence. It should, however, be encouraged to fend for itself and lead as natural a life as possible.

If you take possession of an owlet you should let the police know at once, because owls are protected by law, and it is an offence to keep one unless for the purpose of nursing it.

The owlet should be fed raw meat, any mice you can catch or steal from the cat, or on raw rabbit, or chicken heads. But give it complete freedom of movement so that it can hunt for itself and go away if it wants to.

There are certain things you can investigate when you have a tame owl on the premises. How well can the bird see in daylight? If it's in a tree in daylight, and you twirl a mouse in your fingers, does the bird recognise the prey? Does it fly down to snatch it? How well can it see in a room illuminated by a 500 watt lamp? How often does the bird produce a pellet? Does it drink a lot of water? How often does it bathe?

You can't, of course, judge wild owls by the behaviour of one which is a household pet; but if you encourage your bird to lead a free, self-hunting life, it will give you a lot of pointers.

While watching owls at dusk, during the night, or early in the morning, you will inevitably become interested in other birds and mammals which are active at the same time. What you hear, and see, will naturally depend on where you live.

It's unlikely that you'll spend much time with owls before becoming acquainted with the woodcock, if this bird is on the same ground. There's no reason in the world, of course, why you shouldn't become interested in the woodcock without ever looking at an owl; but where the two live on the same ground your owl-watching will certainly lead you to it.

The woodcock is active at dusk and dawn, just about the time you would be seeking owls. Its display flight, called roding, takes place when the owls are stirring to begin their night's hunting, and when they're breaking off in the morning. The evening flight is the main one.

A roding woodcock flies the same circuit each night. Every bird I have watched has roded anti-clockwise (withershins is the Scots word) and just above tree height. But all woodcock may not do so. The flight is fast but the wing-beats slow and owl-like. The bird's sky silhouette is distinctive.

By sitting on the ground in a convenient place you can easily watch the woodcock's roding flight. It won't be disturbed by your presence on the ground below. Once you know its flight line, you can get close to it if you want to by sitting up in a tall tree with a thick top—for example, a dense spruce or a shaggy-headed pine. I've had woodcock passing six feet from me when I was in a treetop hide watching owls.

During the roding display the woodcock croaks and chirps.

The pattern is several croaks, followed by a chirp, and the complete call is uttered at regular intervals.

No doubt you've heard it said that the woodcock doesn't rode in the morning. Well, this is something you can check for yourself if you get out to the spot before daylight. Many a time, when I've been sitting up a tree watching owls, I've heard the woodcocks croaking on their morning circuit, flying the same course as at night.

If you watch woodcocks carefully—and the best way is

always to be on the spot, hidden, before the birds become active—you'll notice that sometimes a bird will break its flight, dip down through the trees, and strike up its mate. The birds will then chase each other round and round the tree trunks.

After such a chase roding often finishes for the evening, but the male bird is just as likely to top the trees and resume his flight.

Woodcock nest in woodland and scrub, favourite places being under bushes, in bracken, or in deep heather with a growth of birch seedlings. But you'll sometimes find a nest as open as a plover's, in short grass under forest trees, or on a carpet of withered leaves.

There's still much argument about whether or not woodcocks carry their chicks. Only the woodcocks really know the answer, but the evidence is strong that they do. I've no doubt in my own mind that the birds do so at times, for whatever reason.

I've had a woodcock drop a chick at my feet after she had risen higher than my head. But, of course, that could have been because the chick was snagged in the old bird's feathers when she flushed, as often happens with pheasants.

By careful observation you may discover the truth for yourself. The clincher for me was when a friend and I watched a woodcock lead three chicks from a main road early in the morning. The fourth chick was left behind, crouching on the crown of the road. In a few moments the woodcock flew to it, and crouched over it as though to brood it. When she flew to the verge the chick was no longer on the crown. We found all four chicks on the verge when we ran to the spot.

Just about the time you're waiting for owls to begin hunting, or for the woodcock to begin his roding flight, you'll almost certainly hear—if you're in pheasant country—the crowing and drumming of the cock pheasant.

This is the cock pheasant's nightly ritual in the breeding season, when he has hens in the vicinity. What you hear is his familiar crow, together with the vigorous clapping of his wings. The display goes on for some little time. Once you've heard it you can try to find the bird responsible; then, by getting into a tree near the spot, early in the evening, and sitting quite still, you can watch him.

During his display, the cock pheasant stands on tiptoe with his chest puffed out. It has been said that he performs his crowing and wing-clapping in the opposite way from a barndoor rooster. Watch a rooster, then a cock pheasant, and see what you think.

You'll sometimes see the pheasant's display without any preparation, if you come on one accidentally, and you spot him first. But there's something very satisfying about being in position to see a performance you expect and have prepared for. Especially when everything works out to plan.

There's hardly anything about pheasants that you won't see much more easily in an aviary, or on a game farm, but there's a lot to be said for getting to grips with the wild-bred birds. A fight between rival males is one of the things you won't normally see on a breeding farm, because the males are penned separately, with a given number of hens each, and have little opportunity to do so.

The cock pheasant is a bonny fighter, as you'll see when two of them meet, or when one meets a farm cockerel, or a bantam. Then the

Cock pheasant in aggressive display in Spring.

feathers often fly in all directions. A tame cock pheasant
will assault a cat without hesitation.

In this country the cock pheasant is usually polygamous.
But sometimes you'll find a cock with only one hen, and then
you may see him taking a turn on the eggs. Even where
there are plenty of hens you'll sometimes find a cock with
only one.

In his display to a hen the cock parades around her with
one wing spread down to the ground, and his tail fanned out
and tilted. The time to watch out for this display is early
in the season.

A hen pheasant who is well settled on eggs, or who has
chicks tapping the shells, is usually easy to observe at close
quarters, provided you are careful and don't make sudden
movements. She will sit tight even when you are standing
two or three feet from her.

The hen pheasant leaves her nest to feed.

Some hen pheasants will even allow themselves to be stroked on the nest. This isn't a recommendation; merely a statement of fact. When the hen pheasant is on somebody else's ground you shouldn't take liberties with her without permission. Hen pheasants are unpredictable. Some, frightened when they've been sitting only a short time, desert right away. Some will desert when they're hatching off. Others will sit long past the time, until they are weak and emaciated on eggs which will never hatch.

A good place to watch out for pheasants is near poultry houses at a farm, especially those close to woodland. Wild pheasants will often feed with the poultry in the early mornings, and this is when you're most likely to see a clash between a cock pheasant and a rooster. That's when you'll realise what a wonderful fighting machine a cock pheasant can be.

Another good place to watch for pheasants is in a potato field, late in the season, before the potatoes are due to be lifted. The birds like walking in the drills, seeking not only wireworms, leather-jackets, and grubs, but any small potatoes exposed on the ridges.

If you watch pheasants often enough in potato fields you may eventually discover certain associations. Foxes, for instance, sometimes lie up in the drills to ambush unsuspecting birds.

I've seen several pheasants caught in this fashion, and there was the memorable morning when a cock pheasant, resplendent in crimson and gold, exploded from the green shaws minus his head. He didn't fly far. . . .

If you have suitable accommodation, and you keep poultry, it's well worth while to give a bantam some pheasant eggs to hatch ; then you can observe the growth of the chicks through all stages, right up to September when the cocks assume their brilliant plumage.

Pheasants thus reared, although half-tame, become quite wild as adults. But you can, if you like, prove that a pheasant can be made as tame as the household budgerigar. This you can do by taking away a chick at hatching time, and rearing it by hand away from the others. You won't know, of course, whether it's a cock or a hen at that age. Such a pheasant will be absurdly tame, and you will be foster-mother and fellow pheasant to it.

This is the Lorenz principle of imprinting. You will be the first thing the chick sees, so you'll be a pheasant so far as it's concerned. It is for this reason that young mammals tame far better if they're taken before their eyes open.

Note, when you're observing pheasants, the great variety of plumage in the cocks ; the variation is less striking in the hens. Almost all wild-bred pheasants in Britain are mongrels, derived from a mixture of several types.

How often do you see a wild-bred cock pheasant with a green neck and no white ring ? Most of them have a white ring, or part of one, on their necks. This indicates the dominance of one type : the pure-bred ring-necked pheasant known as *Phasianus c. torquatus*.

Another bird active at night in spring is the blackcock.

The blackcock is the male of the black grouse, the female being called the greyhen. The sexes are quite distinctive in plumage. The greyhen is like a large, but less red, red grouse. The blackcock has plumage of ebony, with a brilliant blue sheen. He has a lyre-shaped tail, with a white patch underneath, white spots on his shoulders, and bright crimson wattles.

Black grouse are usually described as birds of the woodland fringe, of the birch scrub and the thickets. This is true, but they're also birds of the open hill at times. While they roost in trees, and fly regularly to and from the forest, the males will display in the open and the greyhen may nest far out on the hill.

If you happen to be out around midnight, watching owls for example, and you hear a sound like the ruckety-cooing of pigeons, you can be sure you're hearing blackcocks on their display ground. You may hear the sound any time from midnight until after sunrise.

In April and May, and in some years into June (as well as at other odd times, as you'll observe) the blackcocks gather on their display ground, which is called a lek. The actual display is called lekking.

There's no great difficulty about watching this display at close quarters, or seeing everything in detail. It's much more difficult to understand the full significance of it. Very probably lekking has more than one function.

When you know you're in a blackcock area you shouldn't have a lot of difficulty finding the birds, for you'll see them

Diagrammatic representation of blackcock on the lek in the month of May.

on the lek by day. If you miss them yourself, you can search over the ground where they've been seen by someone else. There will be feathers lying about the lek, the ground will be trampled where birds have stood or paraded, and there will be droppings all over the place.

A lek varies in area according to the number of birds visiting it. If only three or four are taking part, it may be no more than 25 feet either way. If a dozen or more birds are coming to it, the active area may extend to 25 yards each way, or more.

Quite often you'll find what might be described as a secondary lek near at hand. This is an area to which the birds fly from time to time, for no apparent reason, and where they'll parade for half an hour or so before returning to the main lekking ground.

Watching lekking blackcocks is a matter of getting under cover. The birds themselves aren't shy or suspicious at this time. If there's a wall close at hand, you can get behind this, with some sort of cover built over and around you. If not, build a hiding place in the middle of the lek, or on the edge of it.

My experience has been that the birds won't be upset by a hide, even a big one, if it's built gradually, and of local materials—branches, brushwood, heather and so on. Once the pile of local materials is big and obvious you can get your proper hide up and cover it with the material from the pile.

If you know the position of the lek in advance, build your hide before the birds have begun to display. If they're already visiting it, choose your building times when they're away from it, so that you don't have to put them off.

Blackcocks are often on the lek by day, and you can do your watching then if you like. My experience has been that the daytime performances are a shadow of those which take place between midnight and sunrise. Other observers

Challenging blackcocks photographed at dawn.

have had different experiences. The best plan, clearly, is to visit the lek at different times of the day and night, and compare the behaviour.

If you decide on a night-shift—and that's when you'll find plenty of " atmosphere "—you should arrive at the lek around midnight, certainly before one o'clock in the morning. You may find blackcocks on the lek when you arrive, because sometimes they stay on it all night. The birds will fly away at your approach, but they'll soon come back. All you have to do is get into your hide and sit still.

Before very long you'll hear the whir of wings as the birds pitch in the darkness, and presently they'll begin *coo-rooing* like pigeons. You'll be able to plot the position of each blackcock by his voice, and, before long, you'll make the birds out in the gloom, especially their white seats and the spots on their shoulders.

You'll observe that each bird has his stance—the place he

holds when he's singing and not arguing or jousting with another blackcock. On his stance he croons and crows.

The birds utter a variety of sounds, the common ones being the crooning and a throaty cat-hiss which sounds like *g-whae*.

Periodically, all the birds on the lek will begin leaping up and down, flapping and lurching as though tied to the ground by invisible strings. The reason for this sudden activity is obscure, but quite often it heralds the arrival of a greyhen on the lek.

When blackcocks fight they leap at each other, meeting beak to beat and feet to feet. Often there's much display and challenging without any actual fighting. And often a fight consists of a series of clashes, with few feathers flying and no damage being done. But there are times when the feathers really fly.

You'll probably notice that fights tend to take place between the same pairs of birds. It's a good idea to make a plan of the lek, sketching in the individual stances as the pattern becomes familiar to you, and giving the birds numbers or letters so that you'll know who is fighting whom.

You may find that, nine times out of ten, A challenges and fights with B, C with D, and E with F, but that, once in a while, A will fight with F, B with E, and so on. There's plenty of room for further study of blackcock behaviour, apart altogether from the entertainment provided by the birds, who appear at times to be performing a kind of figure dance.

Birds which have been active during darkness will usually drift away from the lek after the sun is up. They'll return in the afternoon and leave again early in the evening, or they may come and go at short intervals. Birds arriving late in the day may stay all night. Disturbance influences behaviour by day ; during the night the birds are seldom interrupted.

Blackcocks on the lek aren't easily frightened. You may find a bird using your hide as a crowing place. So, on cold mornings, you'll have a certain freedom of movement to rub your hands, twiddle your toes, and otherwise keep yourself warm.

If you're within easy reach of an established lek it's always worth while to keep it under observation throughout the year, because the birds may visit it in October and November, or in March, even when there's snow on the ground.

On a still morning the crooning of blackcocks can be heard a long way off. The sound will lead you to a lek, even on ground that's new to you. Don't imagine, however, that you'll always find a number of birds. Individual blackcocks will croon and crow on their own, at any hour, far from any established lek.

Try to observe something of blackcock behaviour away from the lek. Watch the birds when they're feeding in the morning. Blackcock which were challenging and threatening and sparring a few hours before now feed peacefully together.

Finding the nest of the greyhen isn't easy because she has such a wide choice of sites. She may nest in heather, or in a grass tussock, among scrub or other vegetation, and, like the red grouse, she's a very tight sitter. Any time you see a greyhen feeding you should try to keep track of her with field glasses. You may be able to watch her back to the vicinity of her nest.

If you come on a greyhen in the heather, and she trails away, staggering and turning somersaults, you can be sure she has young close by. A careful search, moving your feet only after your eyes have checked the ground, should find the chicks.

A greyhen flushed from eggs doesn't usually behave in this way, her flight being strong and direct. Distraction display, formerly called injury feigning, is an almost certain indication of chicks. But some greyhens will display from eggs which are in an advanced state of incubation.

If you live in Scotland, or are visiting Scotland in spring, and find yourself near a forest where there are capercaillies, you should make a point of trying to see them. The capercaillie is the biggest grouse in the world.

At one time the bird was found all over Britain. Latterly it was to be found only in Scotland. There it became extinct in 1760, and for 87 years there wasn't a capercaillie in any part of Britain. In 1837 several cocks and hens were introduced to Scotland from Sweden. These birds became established and, with later introductions, were the ancestors of our present stock.

The cock caper is a giant bird—all beetle green and dark blue and brown, with a prominent beard and bright crimson wattles—nearly a yard long. In bulk he's like an eagle. When he flies through the tall forest trees he rattles along like an express train, but it's amazing how such a huge bird can glide and swerve round the trunks without mishap.

Like the blackcock, the capercaillie has a special display, which usually takes place early in the morning, from about two o'clock onwards. By daylight the birds are wandering away from the display area, but individuals may perform on and off throughout the morning. Display takes place on the ground and in trees.

As with blackcocks, the display ground is betrayed by the presence of droppings and feathers. On the ground, the cock caper struts about with his tail erect and fanned out. He holds his head stiffly erect and clicks his beak constantly and rhythmically. He interrupts his parade from time to time with vertical leaps into the air, and vigorous flapping of his wings.

His vocal display is preposterously inadequate for so great a bird. It consists of a low-pitched *tick—tick—tick*, and a sound like the popping of corks. He has other calls, difficult to describe.

Cock capercaillie, the biggest grouse in the world, in full display.

On rare occasions a displaying cock capercaillie becomes aggressive towards human beings. Hence the reports of birds assaulting the postman or barring the path of hikers on quiet forest or hill roads. A bird like this has been killed attacking a Land Rover.

Because of his powerful beak, the cock caper, who takes a dislike to people, is a different proposition from a barn door rooster. His peck can be painful, and damaging. He could take a piece out of you. A bird like this injured my elbow.

But capers like this are rare. The species isn't, by any stretch of the imagination, a predator on man. But you should always be prepared to meet, and never be surprised by, a cock who thinks he owns the forest.

If you're ever confronted by an aggressive cock caper you should try to pass him quietly by. If he begins to crowd you, threatening, tap him under the chin with a stick or slap him smartly across the face with your cap. But get behind a tree, or under cover, if he tries an assault from the air, and wait until he cools down.

Don't, however, get any wrong ideas about capercaillies in general. You could visit capercaillie country every spring for the next twenty years without ever meeting a cock who would stay long enough to be looked at.

Since you will normally be dealing with cock capers who display at each other rather than at human beings, and since the normal birds usually take off at sight of a human being, the best way to get to grips with them is to have a hiding place on the display ground.

You can put up such a hiding place, complete, in an afternoon—and afternoon is the time to do it. Make it of hessian, or some such material, covered with brushwood, pine branches, spruce fronds, heather or bracken, or whatever is lying about the area. If you get into your hiding place early in the morning, about half past two or thereabouts, you should see all there is to see.

The hen capercaillie is a handsome bird, with plumage of buff and white, laced with black. She has a rufous breast. Her great size should distinguish her from other grouse, although you might well mistake her for a greyhen at first.

Most hen capercaillies are woodland nesters, and most nests are close to the base of a tree or tree stump. The birds like sloping ground ; in fact, they seem to prefer woods on hillsides to woods on the flat.

At nesting time, a sitting hen will allow a close approach before she takes wing. You can stand and look at her from a few feet away. But once you've found her there's no need to interview her on her doorstep so to speak. She's big enough to be seen from a distance.

The presence of very large droppings in an area of woodland indicates that a broody capercaillie has been feeding there,

240

Red grouse returning to her nest in the evening after feeding.

so you can begin your search radiating out from that point.

When I'm photographing a hen capercaillie I pick, first of all, an uphill viewpoint, about twenty-five or thirty feet away. There I begin collecting a heap of brushwood. Later I move this heap to where I want it, and later still I make a proper hide under it. From this hiding-place I can watch and photograph the sitting bird.

I like to be at hand when the bird is hatching off, because this is when she utters her soft broody call. Her approach to the nest is usually by way of the trees until she is about fifteen or twenty yards away. Then she flies down to within a dozen feet or so and walks the rest of the way. Considerately treated, a hen capercaillie with chicks can be watched fairly easily at close range.

Make a point of watching capercaillies when they're feeding, in the trees or on the ground. I think you'll find that a caper in a tree is a different bird from one on the ground.

In a tree it is alert and wary, ready to take off at the slightest disturbance ; on the ground it is less wide-awake. It doesn't appear to associate a vehicle with danger, and I've driven right up to three hens feeding on a forest road, stopped, and watched them carry on pecking shoots from a fallen tree.

In capercaillie country, an early morning jaunt in a car or van is a good idea. In this way you'll sometimes see what you might otherwise miss.

Capercaillies feed almost entirely on the shoots of conifers ; they also eat the catkins of the alder. So you would expect to see the birds feeding mostly in trees. And they do. But they also visit cornfields from time to time, to feed on the stooks.

Where this is happening it's a simple matter to arrange a number of stooks into a hiding place. You can get into this before daylight and await the arrival of the capercaillies. If they do come you'll find them easy enough to work with. If they come. . . .

This is when you'll see cock capers as close as you're ever likely to see them, and if you've any ideas about trying to photograph them you might come up with something spectacular. Photographs of British cock capercaillies are still very scarce.

There are two night birds you should make a point of seeking out any time you happen to be in their breeding areas. They're the Manx shearwater and the storm petrel.

If you're visiting the Western Isles of Scotland—for example Eigg or Rum—or Orkney or Shetland, or the Scillies, Skokholm or Skomer, you should make a point of spending a night with the shearwaters. It's at night they fly to their nests, to change over with their incubating partners, or to feed their young.

Manx shearwater at nesting burrow, midnight, island of Rum.

The Manx shearwater is pelagic, which means that, outside the breeding season, it spends its entire time at sea. But it has to come ashore to breed. One of the most spectacular colonies is on a mountain top on the Nature Reserve of Rum.

By day, there's no activity at all on the shearwater breeding grounds. In each nesting burrow there will be a bird sitting on an egg, a bird with a very small chick, or an untended chick. In each case, one bird remains in the burrow with the egg or chick while the other is at sea. Sometimes an incubating bird will sit for two, three or four days at a time. The chick is fed once in twenty-four hours—at night.

The chick is tended by the parents for two months, then deserted. Afterwards it remains in the burrow for up to a fortnight before it comes out and flies to the sea.

Shearwaters don't fly in from the sea until after dark, and

Winter brings the whooper swans from the north to Britain.

they can be watched assembling off-shore to await nightfall. After two or three days at sea, each is carrying a rich cargo of fish-oil for its chick.   In the assembly area the birds can be seen resting on the water, or flying swiftly in ziz-zag flight above it, tilting steeply, with the lower wing-tip almost cutting the surface.

You should visit the shearwater ground before sunset and sit quietly.   You need no cover.   Just sit still.

Once it's dark the birds will arrive.   They'll fly all round you at high speed, wailing and screaming, with no collisions and no crashes.   They weave a bewildering pattern of criss-cross flight.   Eventually all pitch at their burrows and disappear inside.   Before long they're all out again, and soon the breeding ground is deserted for another twenty-four hours.

On nights of bright moonlight the birds may not come to the nests at all. So you have to be prepared for disappointments.

If you want to see a chick you can reach down into a burrow and take one out. You can scrape away enough soil to let your arm reach the nest. But don't use a trowel for the work in case you cut the chick in half. I've heard of this happening with people who ought to have known better.

Other night-flying sea birds are the storm petrel and Leach's petrel. Leach's is a bird of remote places, but the storm petrel breeds in the Western Isles of Scotland, the Orkneys and Shetlands, the Scilly Isles, Skokholm and Skomer, and several Irish islands.

Both species are sometimes storm-blown inland, and may be found, dead or exhausted, in the most unlikely places—far up mountain glens or on the edge of towns. The storm petrel has a white patch on its rump ; Leach's has a forked tail. Both are small, about the size of swallows.

If you sit by the nesting burrows, you'll see petrels flying in at night just as the shearwaters do, and you can have a wonderful night with only the whisper of the sea and the bleating of lambs as accompaniment to this nocturnal display.

You can reach the chick of the storm petrel in the same way as the shearwater's. Most burrows require a little excavation, so be careful not to injure a chick.

When the wild geese arrive in this country in autumn, we're often first aware of them by their voices in the night sky. Their cries have been likened to the music of foxhounds.

It's as winter visitors that we're most familiar with the wild geese in this country, although that needs some qualification nowadays. In the first place there's the world famous collection of wildfowl at Slimbridge in Gloucestershire —a place you must visit if you've any interest in geese at all. Elsewhere, in private collections, other geese breed freely,

and interbreed with other species just as freely. And there are now a number of flocks of Canada geese breeding wild in Britain.

So far as truly wild, native birds are concerned, it's still true to say that we have only the greylag, and that our breeding stock are confined to certain remote parts of Scotland and the Outer Isles, notably the Uists.

If you visit the Uists, naturally you'll want to see geese ; and there's no reason why you shouldn't, so long as you keep in mind that you're dealing with a rare, specially protected bird, and that you should take no liberties.

The wild greylag is a wary, shy and temperamental bird. When nesting it is better left alone. Geese aren't owls and shouldn't be treated as such. Watching a goose with goslings, or geese feeding, are things you can safely do. A scared goose will always come back to her goslings. If you scare a winter flock you lose them for the time being. But there's no harm done.

Wintering geese, generally speaking, feed by day and rest

by night. They flight out at dawn, or earlier, to their feeding grounds—pasture, young grassland, stubble or potato fields, or marshland—then fly back in the evenings to roost for the night on mudflat or loch, depending on area. Often they flight to rest long after dark. And they will flight out to feed in moonlight.

An experienced wildfowler is the man to tell you something of the movements of the grey geese in his area. On the coast he'll tell you about flight times, flight lines, tides and so on. If the geese are near your home you'll work out these things for yourself.

In my own area we get from 100 to 400 greylags each winter. The birds spend the night on a small loch, and feed in the surrounding fields by day. For several winters I had a hide on the shore of the loch, and from it I watched the geese at night, talking and gaggling, flapping and bathing.

Curlew

Woodcock

Sand Martin

Nightingale

I watched them on moonlit nights, too, when they flew to and fro, between the loch and a field nearby.

I never built hides near any of the fields where the geese fed by day, because I could approach most of them unobserved, and hide in a ditch or hedge-bottom when I had arrived. From such watching-places I've had geese under observation for an hour at a time.

It is a waste of time trying to approach feeding geese openly. They'll remain on the ground until you're a couple of hundred yards away, then they'll rise in a body and circle high, laughing at you.

In hard winters the geese on the moor near my home sometimes visit the farm stackyards at night to look for scattered grain or any bite they can find. I've watched them there a few times, but it's an uncertain business. In fact you never really know what geese will do. So much of their behaviour depends on so many things.

Pay close attention to feeding geese. You'll notice that, at any given moment, there will be birds standing like sentinels, with their heads held high, and it's tempting to think of them as such. Certainly they'll give warning of any danger

248

they see. But no sentinels are posted.

Species tend to gather in traditional areas. And they tend to feed in traditional places. The three best known grey geese—the greylag, pinkfoot and whitefront—have their preferences; but you couldn't really lay down hard and fast rules. You might say that the greylag doesn't like potato fields whereas the pinkfoot does, and the whitefront is the bird of inland marshes and old pastures. Greylags like threshy pastures. Both pinkfeet and greylags like young grass.

The greylag nests in a few parts of Scotland, notably the Outer Isles. Their main breeding station is at Loch Druidibeg in South Uist, which is now a Nature Reserve. Here, between 35 and 50 pairs nest each year on islets amongst thick vegetation, and in June many geese with goslings can be seen on Druidibeg or nearby lochans. The greylags of Druidibeg can be watched from the road on flights to their feeding grounds.

There are many birds which are active by night in the sense that they do more than wake up when disturbed. The nightingale sings at night, and is noted for the habit, although the real business of its life takes place by day. The sedge warbler will also sing at night. Grouse call at night. Nesting

249

Cock Capercaillie

Cock Pheasant

Greylag Goose

Nightjar

gulls call throughout the night. The voices of peewit and curlew are part of the fabric of the night in spring and summer. Swifts may spend the short summer night on the wing. But these are all birds which can best be observed by day.

The nightjar is different. This swift-like bird, garbed like an owl, is a night flier. It roosts by day, and comes out with the bats and the owls.

Fern owl is one of the nightjar's names ; goatsucker is another. But it isn't an owl and it doesn't suck goats.

Nightjars frequent fern brakes and heather-clad ground in open woodland, forested hillsides, or heaths near trees. At dusk their *churring* can be heard. It's a distinctive sound, which can be heard on and off during the night. The sound is uttered by roosting birds, not by birds in flight.

The nightjar lays its two eggs on the ground. The bird itself is cryptically marked. On the ground it becomes almost invisible. Roosting along a branch it looks like a bit of bark or an old stick. Its flight is buoyant ; its silhouette is like a swallow's.

You can sit in the middle of a fern brake and watch the nightjars on the wing. And you can build yourself a hide of the local materials—ferns or heather—and watch the bird at the nest from a range of twelve feet or so. Build the hide by day, and get into it before dusk. If you behave quietly the bird won't be alarmed.

You'll have noticed that, throughout this book, I've put the emphasis on watching selected mammals and birds at close range, in may cases using natural or fabricated hiding-places. That happens to be my way. It doesn't have to be yours. But whatever way you choose to do things, there are certain rules you should obey.

When you've visited a nest on the ground, you should smooth back all disturbed vegetation so that you don't leave a plain trail leading to it.

If you climb to a nest in a tree, don't tear away half the cover trying to get your hand to it.

If you're faced with a nest in a spindly tree or bush, don't pull the tree or bush over so that you can see into it. Carry a stick and a small mirror. Tie the mirror to the end of the stick, raise the stick above the nest, and you'll see the contents in the mirror.

Don't jump to the conclusion that a nest has been deserted because the eggs are cold. Leave them for another day. Birds' eggs are cold while the clutch is being built up, and very often cool when the bird is off feeding.

Don't stand or sit in full view of a bird that is calling plaintively, obviously wanting to get back to a nest. Move away.

Don't try to remove tiny eggs from a small nest to look at them—for example, the eggs of willow warbler or wren—because they're fragile and you'll almost certainly break them. There's no point in handling small eggs.

Don't handle the young birds in a nest, because they're liable to quit before they're ready to fly.

Don't visit a nest too often. Once in 24 hours is often enough for all normal purposes of observation.

A way to ensure the safety, from a marauding cat, of a nest in a bush or hedge is to enclose it loosely in big-mesh wire netting. The small birds will get through. I've done this with a yellowhammer's nest from which a magpie had taken a nestling. The rest of the brood survived.

A way to ensure the safety of a nest in a tree is to climb half-way up and tack barbed wire in a spiral all the way down. That'll stop boys from climbing to the nest. It'll stop you too.

A way to prevent rats from visiting your bird table is to have a sloping collar, like a lamp-shade, round the stem just under the top.

A way to save the birds at your table from cats is to have it in an open place and built tall.

Finally : you'll find, I hope, that making the acquaintance of birds, as individuals, is a rewarding and fascinating pursuit. You'll find this, whatever your interest in birds turns out to be—charting distribution, ringing, counting, spotting as many species as you can, species studies, recording arrivals and departures, feeding birds or merely looking at them. Pleasure there should always be, however difficult the species you're interested in.

There's really no limit to where you can go to look for birds, but it's a matter of courtesy to ask the permission of landowners, farmers, market gardeners, foresters and others before you go on their ground. So far as Nature Reserves are concerned, the Nature Conservancy should be consulted about the regulations concerning those you want to visit.

When you're out and about behave like a trustee of the countryside. Consider other people's rights and interests. Don't damage trees or crops. Don't uproot rare plants. Close all field gates. Don't disturb livestock. Don't take a dog on land without permission, and don't let it chase stock or ground game. Have a respect for living things. Respect for life is the first requirement of a naturalist.

BIBLIOGRAPHY

BATTEN, H. M. *British Wild Animals*. Odhams, London.

BURTON, MAURICE. *Animal Legends*. Frederick Muller, London, 1955.

CAMPBELL, BRUCE. *Finding Nests*. Collins, London, 1953.

FISHER, JAMES. *Watching Birds*. Collins, London, 1953.

FITTER, R. S. R. and R. A. RICHARDSON. *The Pocket Guide to British Birds*. Collins, London, 1952. Also *Pocket Guide to Nests and Eggs*. Collins, London, 1954.

HICKLING, GRACE. *Grey Seals and the Farne Islands*. Routledge and Kegan Paul, London, 1962.

HURRELL, ELAINE. *Watch for the Otter*. Country Life, London, 1963.

LEUTSCHER, ALFRED. *Tracks and Signs of British Animals*. Cleaver Hume Press Ltd., London, 1960.

LONDON NAT. HIST. SOC. *The Birds of the London Area since 1900*. Collins, London, 1957.

LORENZ, KONRAD. *King Solomon's Ring*. Methuen, London, 1952.

NEAL, E. *The Badger*. Collins, London, 1948.

NICHOLSON, E. M. *Birds and Men*. Collins, London, 1951.

PIKE, OLIVER G. *Wild Animals in Britain*. Macmillan, London, 1950.

PITT, FRANCES. *Wild Animals in Britain*. Batsford, London, 1938.

SCOTT, PETER and HUGH BOYD. *Wildfowl of the British Isles*. Country Life, London, 1957.

SMITH, STUART. *How to Study Birds*. Collins, London, 1945.

SPEAKMAN, FRED J. *The Young Naturalist's Year*. G. Bell & Sons, London, 1958.

STEPHEN, DAVID. *String Lug the Fox*. Lutterworth, London, 1950. Also *Wild Animals and their Ways*. Collins, Glasgow, 1959.

THOMSON, H. V. and A. N. WORDEN. *The Rabbit*. Collins, London, 1956.

VESEY-FITZGERALD, BRIAN. *It's my Delight*. Eyre and Spottiswoode, London, 1947.

INDEX